Righteous & Rich

RIGHTEOUS & RICH

AND ABRAM WAS VERY RICH IN CATTLE,
IN SILVER, AND IN GOLD (GEN. 13:2)

ED JOHNSON

Righteous & Rich

© 2021 by Ed Johnson.

All rights reserved. This book or any portion thereof may not be reproduced or used in any manner whatsoever without the express written permission of the publisher except for the use of brief quotations in a book review.

Printed in the United States of America.

First printing, 2021.

ISBN: 978-1-7375559-0-2

Unless otherwise noted, all Scriptures marked KJV are from the King James Version of the Bible.

Book Cover Design -The JonMaxx Group, LLC
Interior Design-Marvin D. Cloud
Photographer: Jamel Nickerson of Jimages

For ordering information contact:

Ed Johnson International Ministries
Christ Worship Center
15620 Sellers Rd.
Houston, TX 77060

www.edjohnsonministries.com
info@edjohnsonministries.com

Dedication

*This book is humbly dedicated to all of the current Christian ministries, Christian Foundations, and Christianpreneurs who have tried to break through financially to complete your Divine Mandates.
The Spirit says, "No more struggle;
it's your time for the overflow!"*

Special Thanks

I want to thank first and foremost my Lord, Savior, and soon coming King, Jesus the Christ. It is an honor and privilege to serve on Your Team, working to restore our Father!

Secondly, I want to thank my wife, Marilyn Maxwell-Johnson, for helping to lift me from the dunghill of life, by breathing and speaking life into me again. No one on earth is more responsible for me completing this book and me doing all that I do than you! You taught me to love and trust again, and you unselfishly share me with all who need me. You let me find my way without criticizing, condemning, or becoming disappointed with me when I took wrong turns. You, Mert, are something unique from God (YAMP)!

Lastly, thanks to my four children (Chas, Christal, Tre' (Edward III), and Kyle), my parents (Ed and Erma Johnson Sr.), my gigantic family (Johnsons and Darbys), my god-children, spiritual sons and daughters, members of Christ Worship Center (Houston, Texas), and friends.

I hit a prophetic dry season, and I heard nothing from God for a while. I started working on this book and the prophetic flood gate opened! I did not make an announcement about the subject or what The Father spoke to me. The list would be too long to print the names of all of you who are responsible for the many accurate prophetic words about this book and the work God has called me to perform. I have your words written down, and I'm seeing them come to pass. I honor each of you and look forward to doing my part to help you in ministry. All the glory goes to God! And, to those of you from all over the country, who heard the Spirit say sow financially into this book when you somehow heard about it. I am still overwhelmed to this day. You all were truly Cornelius (Acts 10) to me. All of you are amazing. I have the best family and friends in the whole world...I'm prayin' for ya.

Special thanks to my long-time friends, Rev. Marvin D. and Gwenevere Cloud. I loved working with you during your *Gospel Monthly Magazine* years as much as I have today. I have always loved, respected, and admired you both – thanks, Marvin!

I have had four transformative pastors during my lifetime: the late Rev. A. M. Johnson Sr. (Riverwood Missionary Baptist Church), the late Robert Anderson (Power House C.O.G.I.C.), Bishop Larry Leonard, Sr. (Morning Star FGBC/The Place of Impact Church), and Archbishop Thomas Wallace (New Day Kingdom Assembly of Churches). I will always honor all of you.

Table of Contents

Introduction — 1

1. The Doctrine of Devils — 9
2. What is Rich? — 23
3. Righteous & Rich Abraham — 33
4. The Ancestry — 43
5. Righteous Trouble — 55
6. Unrighteous Rich: Bad Practices — 65
7. No More Reproach — 75
8. The Marketplace — 85
9. Buyers of The Marketplace — 93
10. Restoring Paths — 103
11. Responsibility and Accountability — 113
12. Why Rich Righteous Believers are Needed — 125
13. Children of Covenant — 135
14. Coalitions and Federations — 147
15. Prayers — 159

    About the Author — 167

Introduction

Jesus did become poor, but He did not shy away from the tools of wealth and power He created for this world. The Magi brought Him gold, frankincense, and myrrh. All three items are intrinsically of great value, costly, and used by the rich to accumulate riches. We must be careful not to use the Word of God to empower our flesh or use it as a weapon or tool to disenfranchise any of the citizens of the Commonwealth of Heaven. Jesus becoming poor is different from Him being poor. He had the power to use all of Earth's resources at any time to demonstrate the Kingdom of God. Jesus did this in feeding thousands and thousands and thousands of people at one time, starting with a meager two fish and five barley loaves, and ending with an accumulation of twelve baskets.

Jesus, in poverty, was richer than the wealthiest man who ever lived because of the power He possessed to control Earth's resources. Let's stop playing games with words and ambiguous interpretations. Instead, let's get to work building this international Christian Commonwealth (Community) to improve the lives of our Christian brothers and sisters that have been praying to The Father for relief. We will need millionaires and billionaires to get the work done. We will need righteous and rich saints!

If you are looking for permission from Christian leadership to pursue riches, then you purchased the wrong book. If, however, you are looking for validation to live your Christian life according to precepts of God, and if that pursuit of a Christian life leads you to wealth and riches; you are at the right place. Some may ask, "What is the difference?" It is an easy question to answer because no Scripture speaks to wealth and riches being a sin. However, how you acquire wealth and riches may be a big problem; and if God did not destine you to have wealth and riches, that could be a bigger problem.

To say all rich people are bad is to in essence say all poor people are good. To say that being rich is bad is to say being poor is good. Furthermore, to say all rich people go to Hell is to say all poor people go to Heaven. To hold on to such beliefs is to have a simplistic view of a somewhat complex issue (if being rich or poor is an issue). I say somewhat because if you listen to the Spirit or search the Word, you can find answers. God will judge the rich and the poor. First, for having received or not having accepted Jesus Christ as their personal Savior, and then, the second judgment would be what they did with the body and opportunities God afforded them in life. That is it.

There is no "go straight to" anywhere without just cause. After receiving Christ, both the rich and the poor must learn of Him to traverse this life with the solemn statuettes taught and reinforced by the Spirit of God and are found, purposefully, and not randomly, in the Word of God. In all of its instructions, inspirations, edifications, and warnings, the Bible speaks to both the rich and the poor that they two will know there is no pass for either one because of life's hardships or luxuries.

I specifically wrote this book for those Christians who believe God has purposed them to be Righteous & Rich! I want to dispel the satanic lies that all rich people go to Hell and you must give up your wealth if you were born into money. While the title of this book is eye catching to some and scandalous to others, I knew it was the best one to catch the eye of some to the disdain of others. As the children of God, it is needed for all of us to embrace the truth about financial freedom.

Mostly, the Church has done a good job of sharing Christ with believers as it relates to Him being the *only* way to the Father to obtain eternal life. However, the message for post salvation leaves a lot to be desired. How we occupy until He comes seems to be a great struggle for this generation that was born into opportunities and options. While the New Testament centers around a new message, a new way, a new entity (The Church), and a soon coming King, we must look to the Old Testament for many societal norms and acceptability prescribed by God.

There has always been a group that thought themselves better than others—turning what should be a fair and equal playing field—into a proverbial minefield (and they knew the placement of all the mines). When Jesus declared He came to set the captives free (Luke 4:18), He meant every word. I wrote this book to give you permission to be and become all that the Kingdom of God has destined you to be for the glory of God the Father, including being righteously rich.

The "gospel of prosperity" in and of itself is not entirely false. While it feeds into the narrative of greed and misuse, it also highlights a great need that people must be financially free to move and do those things that will bring comfort and joy to their families, businesses, and personal lives. As with many other things, we do not understand and do not fit into our Christian designer boxes wrapped by cultural denominationalism. Many only seek to rebuke it and not explore it for truth and significance.

We must ask: What is God *really* saying? A knee-jerk reaction benefits no one. Especially, it does benefit those who a satanic force may bind, who the deliverance of God originally intended a truth to be known to and set free from. Let us state a fact that people seem to shy away from; many of our prominent religious leaders are guilty of not being able to identify with the very people God sent them to minister grace. Many people believe salvation is all you need, and you should be satisfied thereafter. I have even heard some quote Paul's exhortation of contentment in Philippians 4:11 as a rebuke of wanting a better quality of life. A person teaching this on TV, radio, or in a book amazes me. The budgets for national TV broadcasting are absolutely mind-blowing. The numbers can range in the millions of dollars annually for a weekly broadcast. It seems okay for those ministries to trust God with the budget, but not okay for the people of God who consume Christian media to strive for a better quality of life.

I am diametrically opposed to the "gospel of prosperity," but I believe that the Gospel of Jesus Christ can free us from the bondage of poverty. I loath the shenanigans I see from time to time in worship services and on Christian TV, as people who *say* they have an anointing for finance endeavor to raise offerings for budgets and projects. We should not deviate from the Word. Ask the people and trust God with the results. No holy water, prayer cloths, or special blessings. Just ask. Just give. Trust God.

Presenting the Gospel in a framework other than a sinner in need of a Savior is an error! The Church should frown upon the initial offering of Christ as a means to fix anything other than a person's soul. Giving Him your life is no guarantee He will deliver you from the trouble in your life.

Salvation is an even exchange: life for life. Jesus saves us, and we live for Him. But I want to make clear in this introduction that human beings do not get to decide how other human beings live for Him. God is the keeper of the thoughts He has for us (Jeremiah 29:11). And the only way to find out the plan He has for you is by praying and walking out your complete salvation.

There is a spirit of oppression in the Church that mirrors the same spirit of Babylon operating in the world. There is a disparity in the Body of Christ; one that delineates the have and have-nots! And the haves are okay with the have-nots being deprived of their inheritance. I often hear and read of those fighting for financial equality in the world refer to the 10% and top 1% who control the world's wealth. Well, there is a 10% and a 1% in the Church who controls Christian wealth – the Christian elites. They, too, are keeping information, opportunity, and resources to themselves. Many are doing this on purpose. Shame on them. And if that is you, know this: You will answer for it in the judgment.

Some have-nots have found their wealth in living deprived lives and preaching a Gospel of sacrifice. If the Lord has called you to a life of poverty, that is fine. But you cannot make poverty a doctrine. Poverty does not get you a seat at the Banquet Table of Christ. He will still judge your works to check the purity of your motives to see why you did what you did with your poor life. Neglecting your earthly assignments for ministry is as derelict as the converse (neglecting your ministry for financial prosperity). Ask the servant in Matthew 25 who received the one talent. There should not be an affluent Jesus and a disenfranchised Jesus: Just Jesus.

While I write this book, our nation grapples with ethnic groups rising against ethnic groups. I have been encouraging the sheep I pastor to be careful of being drawn into the world's chaos because it is the prophetic timetable of God, spoken by Jesus Himself, for identification and warning to the Church of His return. I am extremely careful because the same issue being addressed and fought in the world is present in the Church and the world has no problem pointing out our hypocrisy. As I see ministers of God fighting for equality in the world, I cannot help but wonder if, just maybe, they got tired of waiting for their counterparts to embrace them in the Church. I often hear the testimony of the singer Helen Baylor, "We all want to be loved." I am not confused. We are still struggling with the unity of the faith because of our dogmas, but if we look closer, we will see affluent people who embrace our doctrine.

We attended seminaries with them and studied with them, but they will never invite us to speak at their church because our presence represents an uncomfortableness their congregants are not ready to deal with. As long as we stay in our places assigned to us by them, they are all right. But, any attempt to improve our quality of life, based on a Scripture we believe frees us from abject poverty, is met with resistance and derision. They label us with terms like heretic, deceiver, false prophet, etc. Well, let me give you a label: satanist!

Jesus said the thief comes to steal, kill, and destroy (John 10:10). Anyone working, directly or indirectly, to keep a person from their inalienable rights to pursue a better quality of life in the Kingdom of God operates with a satanic spirit. They aid Satan in his plan to prevent the Church from the missions Christ has called her to complete on His behalf (1 Corinthians 15:28).

Influential church leaders, connected to powerful politicians and highly regarded by political parties, have interconnected the gospel of prosperity and the "message of prosperity." They have broadly brushed the subject, so anyone who would dare speak of opportunity, promotion, and increase to the people of God is immediately castigated. Satan, The Lord rebukes you! From this day forward, you will no longer control the message, and your attempts to control the results will fail miserably. We are rising to take back our inheritance as becoming the Children of God. You are the thief. And, those in the Church who have aligned themselves with your ungodly intentions to keep segments of the Body of Christ impoverished or relegated to the working class will be stripped of their stations, influence, and power; in Jesus' name.

As we move to the first chapter, I want to be clear with you regarding my intentions. This book is not about greed (the insatiable appetite for money and power). It is a brief look at those God-believing ancestors who had money, and power, how they handled it, and what we can learn from them. Some did well with money and power, and some did poorly. Open your heart and mind to the fact that some of you God has called to be well off, rich, and *very* rich for purposes that He alone can communicate with you and provide you with the grace to carry out that mission. Learn from those who did well and those who did not do well.

Israel needed wealth to establish nationhood and survival as there were no other people on the planet Earth with their unique God-given purpose. It was a cornerstone of its covenant with God. The Church also needs it! Especially now. Some Christian individuals with wealth and riches are selective or prejudiced in their missionary work. Unless they fit the demographic of their comfort level, then peoples, nations, and continents are left out. We do not have time to call meetings, state our case, and negotiate. Let God raise you, believer, for the people He has called you to reach. Live a righteous and rich life before your God and the people.

CHAPTER 1

The Doctrine of Devils

What is the doctrine of devils? Plainly stated, it is a biblical principle in which demonic beliefs or teachings are introduced to the Church to thwart the faith of people who believe in Jesus Christ.

1 Timothy 4:1-3 King James Version states: "¹Now the Spirit speaketh expressly, that in the latter times some shall depart from the faith, giving heed to seducing spirits, and doctrines of devils; ²Speaking lies in hypocrisy; having their conscience seared with a hot iron; ³Forbidding to marry, and commanding to abstain from meats, which God hath created to be received with thanksgiving of them which believe and know the truth."

The above passage does not contain an exhaustive list of the teaching but rather a few examples of the dangerous web of deceit, and more concerning, the cruel effect on the believer. Holy Spirit speaks through Paul to our generation, telling us to be on guard and that we would be able to identify the "latter times" by an exodus from the Church precipitated by a demonic undertow. Holy Ghost said these teachings, directly inspired by demons, introduced to people, and then taught to unsuspecting Christians, will cause Christians to forsake Christ. Some teachings are overt, questioning the deity of Jesus Christ and Holy Ghost. Some are subtle, like salvation through the sinner's prayer alone, infinite grace, popular teachings on destiny, or Christian Yoga. Suppose we are not careful, prayerful, and filled with the Spirit. In that case, we can find ourselves embracing demonic teaching – which is nothing but a satanic strategy to overthrow the faith of believers, and land them in the pits of Hell.

I believe that the Church has embraced demonic teaching and caused confusion, frustration, and even generational discouragement. What is that teaching? That being rich is inherently evil. In some sectors, the belief looks like a total abandonment of so-called worldly pleasures – which is typically associated with money and all the accouterments money can buy–it is embracive of the poverty vows. Others believe in the hazards of wealth but only when the wealth is not in their hands. It is better when the wealth is distributed and managed by them. Many of them are the product of generational wealth or have broken the cycle of poverty through education, entrepreneurialism, investments, and local chambers of commerce; organizations that promote networking and partnerships. Many of the poor herald their poverty as a virtue and believe it will get them a special place in Heaven. In contrast, many of the rich go to church on Sunday and send their money overseas, if at all, to help people they never have to touch or see face to face. Even in that regard, their money works for them.

It is imperative to understand how we got here to adequately address the issue of systemic poverty in the

Body of Christ. Human beings have taken liberty with the Word of God, teaching the people of God patterns that are not of God. While we dissect Scripture for its proper interpretation, the whole Bible must still reflect a complete story or instrument. When we do that, we should all come to the same conclusion: Where is the God of Abraham, Isaac, and Jacob? If we look at the Body of Christ as a whole and not judge it by our group or personal experiences, we should see the Body of Christ in want. Not of any neglect on Christ's part, but rather our appropriation of the Scriptures in totality and fairness. There is an element of The Abrahamic Covenant that has not increased the span of the Body of Christ. Money! It is an extremely sensitive subject for many reasons, but I will do my best to bring a Kingdom perspective to ignorance and inequality concerning Christian wealth. Somebody must address the optics of Christian haves and have-nots and address why there seems to be Christian economic oppression or at least callousness.

Several years ago, I accompanied a family member who had to sing at one of the prominent Caucasian churches in our city. Before the Sunday performance, it was required to meet with the sound team and have a soundcheck. While they waited on the team to finish up a meeting, I looked around. Having never visited their campus before, I was quite intrigued. I noticed outside of the door to the main sanctuary, they were in the midst of a fundraising campaign. I cannot remember what the project was for, but the goal was in the millions. They had reached a couple of million dollars, and I wanted to know how long the campaign had been in effect. After I asked the sound guy about it, I was shocked! He said the campaign had recently started; I was looking at the initial commitments made from the previous Sunday's offering. On the inside, I was astonished, but I refused to show it. He went on to say, without any hint of arrogance or disrespect, "We'll have that campaign completed by the end of the month," and he never noticed or acknowledged my presence again.

As I rode home, my mind was totally discombobulated. What had I experienced? I come from a part of the Kingdom where campaigns last for months and even years. In some cases, the projects never finished during the pastor's tenure or lifetime and were a source of embarrassment. The financial struggles were real.

I could not reconcile in my mind that which I had seen with where I came from. I never attended a church with an edifice in disrepair or of which I was ashamed. Neither had I attended a church that was anywhere close to the aesthetic excellence and financial well-being of that church either. Here is where my mind experienced a great disconnect: The church was made up of Christian people. It was not about the building but the building spoke loudly about the people's lives and prosperity. I am melancholy by nature, therefore it does not take much to activate disappointment, discouragement, and despair in me. I went down. I could only thereafter internalize grief from that moment because I had no answers to the question: What is wrong with us?

After all of these years, this is my conclusion: There are devils in the church, especially in the pulpits. And it has nothing to do with race but an evil intent of their actions. There is something innately evil about a person with their foot on someone's neck, but it is also evil for others to stand by and watch and consent as it happens. If the Gospel you hear on Sunday, the teaching you receive at Bible Study, coupled with your personal Bible Study frees you from seeing about your neighbors, you have not heard the Gospel message of Jesus Christ. You have not applied His Word, and you are not filled with Holy Ghost! You either hear demonic messaging or your consciousness is seared. You are in danger of Hell's flames.

Luke 16:24 -25 states, "[24]And he cried and said, Father Abraham, have mercy on me, and send Lazarus, that he may dip the tip of his finger in water, and cool my tongue; for I am tormented in this flame. [25] But Abraham said, Son, remember that thou in thy lifetime receivedst thy good things, and likewise Lazarus evil things: but now he is comforted, and thou art tormented."

Not having the capacity to relieve the sufferings of others could have eternal ramifications. I am aware of many affluent churches with huge Overseas Mission budgets, but you do not see them with a stateside footprint in inner-city areas. As a child, I had it drilled over and over in my head, "charity starts at home and then spreads abroad." God placed Lazarus right outside the gate of the rich man – he saw him every morning and every night but did nothing about his plight. The rich man did not go to Hell because he was rich but rather because he refused to do something to help Lazarus. For believers who experience wealth, this book may be a call of activism on your part. Believers who come from some level of financial independence can find it exceedingly difficult to understand the plight of those who aspire to such freedom. Neither do they understand the mental and spiritual roadblocks that can render one exhausted to the point they end up opting out of the process, although they still hold on to their faith in God. This book is a call to arms. Many of you who fall in that category of not understanding will be called on by the Spirit of God to minister (help) to individuals endeavoring to provide their families with a better quality of living. The knowledge you have received of the world will be invaluable, as we are still connected in many ways to the world's system. The financial education and experience you have received will become your ministry.

 I can only pray that after reading the introduction, you can feel my heart in the Spirit. If you have not read the introduction, please do so before you consume the rest of this information. Why? We have some real issues that need addressing, and I do not want you to think I am a critic of the Church or I operate with a spirit of envy. I am genuinely concerned about our Lord's Church. Some of us live in isolation because of locality, denomination, or personality, and sadly because of our prejudices. No matter the cause, it should not be in God's Church. Jesus prayed for oneness, for unity (John 17:11, 21-23). In his revelatory letter to the Church at Ephesus, Paul told us to aspire for unity of the faith (Ephesians 4:13). If we are to achieve this goal, we must be strong enough to self-critique as well as self-correct. One evening, one of my former pastors had a guest speaker. My pastor had such regard for this man's studiousness of the Bible, and he held a Q & A after the evening session. Someone asked a question on a subject that my pastor had previously taught, but they were unaware, and my pastor did not readily agree with the response of the guest minister. It contradicted my pastor's teaching. My pastor went to the microphone and probed the guest minister until he was satisfied that he was wrong and the guest minister was correct. In front of the entire church, my pastor said, "I stand corrected!" I thought it was impossible to gain any more respect for him (my pastor) than that which I already had, but to see him handle correction in a public forum with such humility set a paradigm in me that I still regard today. You are never too old or too smart to learn. Sometimes we are too proud to change. This is what the devil, the enemy of our souls, depends on as he continues to spew his doctrine among us.

While specifically, we are looking at the believer and riches in this book, without hesitation, I submit to you that there is an overall problem with the educational arm of the body of Christ. And because the teaching is incomplete, the preaching is incomplete. Subsequently, the living is incomplete. There are many opinions, interpretations, and beliefs.

Instead of believers' continual growth in the Word, there seems to be more of a looking for a place to anchor and dry dock. This glorious Gospel should be a lifetime of delving into and searching led by and inspired by Holy Ghost. Any revelation that Holy Ghost has not inspired will bring weakness to the Faith, to the believer, to the

Church. It will serve to castrate and not yield fruit that will remain. Jesus rebuked the people because they altered the Word.

In Matthew 15:4-8 we read, "⁴ For God commanded, saying, Honour thy father and mother: and, He that curseth father or mother, let him die the death. ⁵ But ye say, Whosoever shall say to his father or his mother, It is a gift, by whatsoever thou mightest be profited by me; ⁶ And honour not his father or his mother, he shall be free. Thus have ye made the commandment of God of none effect by your tradition. ⁷ Ye hypocrites, well did Esaias prophesy of you, saying, ⁸ This people draweth nigh unto me with their mouth, and honoureth me with their lips; but their heart is far from me."

God commanded one thing, but somebody, some person, decided the commandment of God should be improved, thereby ignoring the command and creating a rule regarding parental relationship they thought to be more suitable. Do not get this twisted! Somebody said, "God has it wrong!" And the keepers of the Word signed off on it.

"Who are you, O man to answer back to God? (Romans 9:20)." You only get demonic doctrine when there is a collaboration between arrogant humans and intelligent demons. This unique partnership can exist by omission or commission. Either way, the plan of God has been diverted or aborted. I cannot understand for the life of me, why ministers are not more careful and fearful of getting it wrong. I know you understand careful, but let me clearly ascertain fearful for you:

Acts 18:24-26 states, "²⁴ And a certain Jew named Apollos, born at Alexandria, an eloquent man, and mighty in the Scriptures, came to Ephesus. ²⁵ This man was instructed in the way of the Lord; and being fervent in the spirit, he spake and taught diligently the things of the Lord, knowing only the baptism of John. ²⁶ And he began to speak boldly in the synagogue: whom when Aquila and Priscilla had heard, they took him unto them, and expounded unto him the way of God more perfectly."

Apollos had the charisma, opportunity, and zeal, but he lacks part of his information. No doubt he could rouse the crowd. In the making of disciples, Apollos fails because he does not have the ability, through his preaching, to provide a word that will set the people free. Why? His information was not complete! We must contemplate the impact our preaching, teaching, and exhortations have on the people of God. What we give them should set them on a road of freedom and keep them on that road. What we provide the people of God should never be lackluster or void of the power that still saves [rescues, delivers, sets free].

Far too many of our pastors and religious leaders have put it on cruise control. A hunger for Truth of The Word is missing in our pulpits. The pews are empty because the leaders are empty. Moreover, we do not have enough Christian leaders who know how to rekindle the flame of the Spirit that should burn in all of our hearts. Some don't know there should be a flame (Matthew 3:11, Luke 3:16). Because the people do not know the difference or because the people don't want the Truth, it gives those leaders permission to not dig or allow them to think they have dug enough. Remember, the words we preach and teach give way to eternal repercussions. Somebody is in Hell right now because a pastor, a minister, or evangelist, gave into the devilish partnership by not preaching and teaching the whole counsel of God. What they do with the Word you minister is not your responsibility; however, what you minister does fall directly in your purview.

I am not calling Apollos an enemy of the Gospel, but I am saying his preaching during that time did not serve the Kingdom well. He preached about a Jesus that would come. But that Jesus had already arrived, died, was resurrected, and now sat on the right hand of the Father. There was no glory in the old message of John. The Way had been prepared, filled, and people lived in it. Apollos did not know it, but he was an unwilling participant in a strategy Satan has used since the days of Adam.

It's called misinformation. It was just enough to be correct and omitted enough to be wrong. It was enough to inspire but not enough to empower. What hope does Apollos provide other than frustration that the people are still in waiting mode via his message? Remember, this is not a criticism but a critique. We as the Church should stay away from these types of scenarios.

But the Spirit sent the husband-and-wife team, Aquila and Priscilla; they took him in, taught him, and perfected or completed his message. Now, Satan could not use him by way of omission any longer. He is no longer an instrument in Satan's toolbox used against the Church while in the Church.

At worst, we can call this an omission by Apollos because of his incomplete knowledge. However, there is another group that we deal with today, and their actions are not accidental at all, but deliberate – commission. They have been sent by their father, the devil, to subvert the faith of the saints of God. These dastardly deeds were told to us by Jude as he addressed them during his ministry, and things have only progressed until our time. It is hard for the laity to wrap their brains around the fact that Satan has a people, too! Not all of them are worshiping him in goth appearance. Many of them worship at home upon their evil altars after they have praised and worshipped with us in church. More disturbing is their continual rise in the ranks of Christendom and they now lead individuals in their reformations and colleges. Yes! They are deceitful workers in the Body of Christ, and with no spiritual discernment, which is only possible through a gift of The Spirit. We often cannot recognize them. They are deceitful workers in the Body of Christ, and it will take the Spirit of God revealing them to us (discerning of spirits) and to give us the strategy to stop their evil work.

Can you see it yet? What else would explain their angry response to the Gift of The Spirit? They want to stay concealed to continue their evil work.

These people have set policy, procedures, and doctrine for many churches to function systematically in concert. Nobody deviates from the designated script, and in some cases, it has been that way for many centuries. They have also forged and fostered relationships with politicians and corporate leaders to further their systemic circle of power throughout the ages, centuries, decades, and years. They have done all this with an outward appearance of gentleness, but they are salivating wolves inwardly. The devil is their father. Their mission is twofold: oppress and prepare. The anti-christ structure must be thoroughly vetted, tested, and controlled before his reveal. How is it controlled? By restricting the knowledge of the people, they limit the success of the people.

The people who speak against Christians receiving wealth and riches are the same ones who are wealthy or rich themselves. They govern with great power and influence, capable of changing secular law or church policy depending on how their bottom-line is affected. There are foundational Scriptures that should have been introduced to us as believers, but they omitted or watered them down. I remind you of the Emancipation Proclamation signed by President Abraham Lincoln, that freed the slaves, but Texas slaves did not know and stayed enslaved longer than they needed to be. I have read, heard, and studied many of the "great" Christian leaders, some considered as preeminent. These gospel elites have no messages on a Christian free enterprise system, financial freedom, or financial equality. How could we get this wrong for so long? We see churches that are financially independent but never make the connection that such economic freedom should encompass the Body of Christ and not be exclusive to a particular group, organization, or gender.

Let me conclude this chapter with this stark observation for my white brothers and sisters. You may not be aware of it, but many of you have been taught partial truth in order for you not to upset the applecart. Please do not think that this is about systematic racism meant to corral people of color. It is also responsible for many prejudices within your white Christian culture. Those oligarchs within our sphere despise your regional accents, clothing attire, middle class, and poor lifestyle. They see you as good for nothing more than serving them on meager salaries. They will never associate with you. They will receive your tithe, offerings, and any help you can be to their church programs. But to be respected and accepted on their level? Never! You, too, must be kept in your place as being beneath them.

Let us agree now that the current system of Church organization and government will implode, and give way to the children of God who will give the Father the fruit due Him in season. Let us pray that God will unleash a judgment upon those leaders who are jealous of Christ's reign and those evil workers who have intruded upon holy ground to disrupt the redemption plan. Let's believe God together to unmask every wolf and expose every angel of light that is not His. Let us decree together: The gates of Hell shall not prevail against the Church of our Lord, Jesus Christ any longer.

CHAPTER 2

What is Rich?

There is no need to beat around the bush. Rich is rich! I have no Greek or Hebrew definition that will bring any new insight, nor is there any parsing of words that would lead to an eisegesis of the word or the concept. I don't have to. Do you know why? Because being rich is not a sin. No Scripture supports God's displeasure with being rich. Nor can you use the life of Jesus as the quintessential example of God's preference in the matter, especially since Jesus was the benefactor of a rich believer's power and influence. (We'll discuss Joseph of Arimathea later.) There is nothing inherently wrong with being rich.

The first time the word rich is used in the Old Testament is in reference to Abraham, prior to his name change. And the Scripture does not only speak of his abundance but also delineates it for the reader for a better understanding of his riches.

In Genesis 13:2 we read: "And Abram was very rich in cattle, in silver, and in gold." The word "very" is an adverb that is used to provide further emphasis on the verb it is modifying. The word very means in a high degree, extremely, exceedingly. So, there is rich that could be described as lower in degree, nominal, and barely but the Word of God speaks of Abram (at the time) as having an overabundance of livestock, silver, and gold. It was not a temporary wealth or a wealth that he was holding for someone temporarily. It belonged to Abram—parts of the wealth was earned—parts were given to him. It all belonged to Abram. Look at the next chapter and verses to see that from chapter 13, Abram's wealth grew more exceedingly, and the delineation is more significant, also.

Genesis 24:34, 35 states, "[34] And he said, I am Abraham's servant. [35] And the Lord hath blessed my master greatly; and he is become great: and he hath given him flocks, and herds, and silver, and gold, and menservants, and maidservants, and camels, and asses."

The word used to describe Abraham's wealth now is the word "great." It could be said that Abraham's wealth is now greatly overabundant. Think massive. The list of things that he holds in abundance has grown also.

Before, there was no mention of flocks, herds, camels, asses, or servants. He very well could have had them, but they could not be classified as overly abundant. At this point in his life, Abraham's riches are enormous. His abundance is abundant. And none of us have a problem with it as we revere him as the father of faith, the example of having a consistent trust in God. There is no Scripture to suggest that God had any problems with Abraham being very rich, especially considering the fact that it was God who blessed Abraham.

While we do not know the exact net worth of Abraham, because there is no specific number ascribed to the list of things in chapter 13, there had to be a noticeable numerical increase because the servant in chapter 24 does not only call his master blessed, but refers to him as being greatly blessed by God. The servant appreciates what we cannot see. Exponential increase! Abraham is not only doing all right for himself; he has become a small town to himself. He manages an empire. With this type of wealth, Abraham can set prices, develop, and move markets. He is his own economy. He can swallow up competitors, outlast his competitors, and deny his competitors. He is self-contained. For that reason alone, he must have help to maintain such a vast structure and organization.

Abraham was so rich he needed to hire people to see after his riches. Did you overlook the word needed? For Abraham to maintain his vast personal economy, let us try to guesstimate what his help would look like. He must have enough men to see after all of the different beasts on a daily basis and have the ability to house and feed them and possibly their families. The Word does not allude to barns or any type of shelter, therefore, there would have to be enough men to rotate out during the night to keep the flock from nightly predators. He also has to compensate them to the degree that includes their loyalty to keep them protecting his empire without becoming jealous and possibly siding with an enemy or undermining his success. There would have to be enough men to protect everyone from a possible invasion from an enemy should there be an attack. We see this when Abraham goes to rescue Lot and has an encounter with Melchizedek. We also get some idea of the number of men with the constant conflict between Lot's staff and Abraham's staff.

Water and grazing is a must. The land must be able to support all livestock all of the time. The livestock mentioned by the servant in chapter 24 are all vegetarians. What is the property line of this estate? How many acres is this place? As massive as it is, it all belongs to Abraham. He is what the world calls filthy rich!

We have only, to this point, talked about Abraham's cattle, but the Word says he is equally excessive in silver and gold. Abraham is not struggling with trying to support the massive number of cattle present on his land. He has what we will refer to as the money to back it up. Abraham has prestige hosting such a large number of cattle, but the money (silver and gold) brings options and power. If necessary, if the land failed, he has the means to acquire additional resources or even move the entire operation. He is not restricted to an unfruitful place, nor does he need to downsize until times got better.

Now this will be a little scandalous to some of you. Please understand the point I am making as Abraham is the progenitor of our faith: There is no Scripture to support Abraham having a great ongoing outreach ministry or that he sold all he had to distribute the proceeds to the poor. If we are to understand righteously rich, we must have an authentic understanding of the Scriptures. I have even heard atheists quote the story of the young ruler when they try to discredit some televangelists because of their extravagant lifestyle. You cannot use that Scripture for that purpose. (We will discuss that in a later chapter.) If being rich was an issue with God, why did He bless Abraham with riches? And, if he was to sell everything, give it to the poor, and live like a pauper, why does the Scripture not give us that account of Abraham's obedience?

Conversely, neither do you see Abraham hoarding his wealth for himself or using it to take advantage of people. We do, however, see the heart of Abraham at least four times that I think deserves mentioning in the context of him being a good pattern for us to follow.

Abraham has the temperament needed to sustain both wealth and its increase. It is a matter of attitude. Do you have the self-discipline required in order to maintain both your soul and your wealth? Even in the secular world, there are many people who desire wealth, but they do not have the necessary discipline needed for such a responsibility. It is not as simple as having the money; it is making sure the money innately does not have you.

Let us look at a few examples of Abraham's character to examine ourselves to see if we could possibly qualify for being righteously rich. We see the patience of Abraham as conflict arises between his workers and the workers of his nephew, Lott.

Genesis 13:7-9 tells us: "⁷ And there was a strife between the herdmen of Abram's cattle and the herdmen of Lot's cattle: and the Canaanite and the Perizzite dwelled then in the land. ⁸ And Abram said unto Lot, Let there be no strife, I pray thee, between me and thee, and between my herdmen and thy herdmen; for we be brethren. ⁹ Is not the whole land before thee? separate thyself, I pray thee, from me: if thou wilt take the left hand, then I will go to the right; or if thou depart to the right hand, then I will go to the left."

Keep in mind, the favor of God is upon Abraham, and not Lot. Abraham's response to this matter, is teaching for us who desire God to increase our lives. He does not seek to curse or destroy Lot, as this could have been an ongoing issue for Abraham. He could have just blown his top, reminded Lot why he is where he is and that he (Abraham) is responsible for his great success. But, no. To the contrary. Abraham humbles himself and seeks to provide a peaceful, harmonious solution for the both of them and he trusts God with the outcome. He defers to Lot in making the decision of direction, knowing that Lot could actually choose the better of places to dwell for his continued success. It did not matter; Abraham was not mean-spirited and vindictive, but a man of peace. Let us be sure to learn this lesson.

After Abraham defeated the federation of nations, we see something unique—generosity—an expression of devotion we have not seen before.

We read in Genesis 14:18-20, "[18] And Melchizedek king of Salem brought forth bread and wine: and he was the priest of the most high God. [19] And he blessed him, and said, Blessed be Abram of the most high God, possessor of heaven and earth: [20] And blessed be the most high God, which hath delivered thine enemies into thy hand. And he gave him tithes of all."

While the Scriptures do not give us more information on Abraham's financial expressions to God, we see here a new expression between the man and the priest. Of all the plunder from this battler, Abraham gives Melchizedek ten percent. Melchizedek did not require it or even suggest the transaction. Verse 20 definitively states that Abraham gave us another lesson to learn as being righteously rich. No one should have to require nor suggest to us. We should not be transactional people but we should initiate. Abraham heard the blessing proceeding from the priest's mouth and was then moved to give ten percent of what he currently had received. This example went on to become a law of God because of the hardness of men's hearts.

I present this last glimpse into Abraham's character, which occurred upon Sarah's death. The Scripture bears record that Abraham was considered a man of stellar reputation, a mighty prince. He was honored among these strangers of which he now resides. He needed a burial plot for Sarah.

Genesis 23:11-16 states, "[11]Nay, my lord, hear me: the field give I thee, and the cave that is therein, I give it thee; in the presence of the sons of my people give I it thee: bury thy dead. [12] And Abraham bowed down himself before the people of the land. [13] And he spake unto Ephron in the audience of the people of the land, saying, But if thou wilt give it, I pray thee, hear me: I will give thee money for the field; take it of me, and I will bury my dead there. [14] And Ephron answered Abraham, saying unto him, [15] My lord, hearken unto me: the land is worth four hundred shekels of silver; what is that betwixt me and thee? bury therefore thy dead. [16] And Abraham hearkened unto Ephron; and Abraham weighed to Ephron the silver, which he had named in the audience of the sons of Heth, four hundred shekels of silver, current money with the merchant."

Abraham could have taken advantage of the offering made by Ephron and, after hearing what the land was worth, haggled the price with him. But it was more important for Abraham to be fair with the people than take advantage of their kindness and respect, even during his personal time of grieving. The one woman he started this journey with has died, but Abraham's character is still in place. We all know of Christian people who death brought the worse out of them. Abraham clearly understood the power associated with wealth. More specifically, he understood the responsibility of righteously rich people in always being a blessing in business, even during emotional times. Bowing himself before them, he paid the stated market price, while grieving for the love of his life. What an example of Christian faith.

Lastly, let us discuss the most powerful element of being rich. Are you ready? Here it is: Abraham does not need to pray for breakthroughs, miracles, or help on a daily basis. This is a level of life most believers have not experienced and those who have, tend not to respect the prayers, needs, hopes, and desires of those who want a better quality of life. Through God's providence, Abraham was set on a path of influence and prosperity that never required him to entreat God once concerning a bill, desire, or misfortune. Some of you cannot imagine that kind of life, and some can imagine not having that kind of life. It existed, and it exists today, not only in the world but also in the Church. Some believers were born into generational wealth. They do not know what it is to struggle financially or to be deprived of any luxury in life. They are like father

Abraham. They are generous, loyal, and equitable people who God has blessed and continues to bless.

Their wealth does not come through ill-gotten gain, and The Father continues to bring increase into their lives. There is nothing wrong with them having access to such financial power, and there is nothing wrong with you working the gifts God has given you and asking The Father to bless the work of your hands which will allow you to experience a life with no financial challenges. Abraham is the model. It existed.

If this is not inspiring and liberating enough, read two verses about his son, Isaac.

Genesis 26:12-13 reports, "[12] Now Isaac sowed in that land, and reaped in the same year a hundredfold. [13] And the Lord blessed him, and the man became rich, and continued to grow richer until he became very wealthy."

If being rich was a sin, the God of Abraham and Isaac is responsible for causing these two men to breach His Word. Of course, that would never happen. Rich means rich. How soon can it happen? Well, God can do anything, but according to the above passage, it happens for Isaac after one 365 day cycle. My encouragement to you is to work the gifts and talents that Father God has given to you, follow peace with all men, be fair with all men in all things, and give to people with no strings attached. If God chooses to increase you financially, you can do nothing about that. Don't apologize for it. Follow the example of your righteous and rich father, Abraham, as his son did.

CHAPTER 3

Righteous & Rich Abraham

For us to understand, appreciate, and duplicate the *Abrahamic pattern*, we must see him as a man of like passion. He must be like us. If not, we will think that the pattern out of reach. If we think the pattern unattainable, the entire *Messianic ministry of Jesus could be severely impacted as Abraham is the prototype*. We must see Abraham as a man and not as God. God implies perfection and autonomy. That is a pattern we are incapable of producing. While Abraham did not stagger at the promises of God (Romans 4:20), that does not imply by any means he was perfect. The father of faith, ever celebrated and rightfully revered, reaches icon status but is unworthy of godly adoration.

Too many Christians make the Peter mistake of seeing patriarchs on the same level as Jesus (Matthew 17:4). Yes, Abraham is listed in the Faith Hall of Fame (Hebrews 11), but he was a flawed individual like the others. We must remember that Abraham was a worshipper of God. For all of his greatness, Abraham was messed up like us. Abraham was messed up, righteous and rich, and there is no law of Scripture precluding you from following the same pattern as Father Abraham.

Abraham starts walking with God at the spry young age of 75. He is void of the voice and existence of God for 75 years. There is too much romancing of Abraham by preachers, and it has had a negative impact on the people. Yes, he hears the voice of God speaking to him about the destiny He has planned for his life and Abraham makes the best decision of his life by choosing to leave home. That one great decision is not the sum-total of Abraham's life.

Broad brushing his life with the success of his first significant step of faith does a disservice to the saints. God reveals to the author of Genesis, Moses, moments that were not so great, moments I am sure Abraham chided himself. They were embarrassing moments. You are already in the pattern. You, too, have made some Hall of Fame decisions coupled with a blooper reel. Some people hate me saying such things, but you, too, are like Abraham. He was a human being like you. At times he got it right, and at other times, he got it wrong.

At the age of 75, he is well past the formative years. Some would say he's at the age where you can't teach an old dog new tricks. By now, mindsets and patterns are well baked. He has to learn the ways of God while simultaneously navigating and managing his habits and his mind. This is the context in which Father Abraham should be presented to his children, for them to know, with all of their weaknesses and flaws, they fit seamlessly into his pattern. If God can use Abraham in such a condition, He can use you, too. And, if He would dare make Abraham righteous and rich, He can do that for you, too!

The first weakness we see in Abraham's character comes right after his first significant step of faith. Upon arriving in Canaan, God confirms Abraham's faith, but famine in the land requires Abraham to leave Canaan and go to Egypt.

In Genesis 12:10-20, we read:

"¹⁰And there was a famine in the land: and Abram went down into Egypt to sojourn there; for the famine was grievous in the land. ¹¹ And it came to pass, when he was come near to enter into Egypt, that he said unto Sarai his wife, Behold now, I know that thou art a fair woman to look upon: ¹² Therefore it shall come to pass, when the Egyptians shall see thee, that they shall say, This is his wife: and they will kill me, but they will save thee alive. ¹³ Say, I pray thee, thou art my sister: that it may be well with me for thy sake; and my soul shall live because of thee. ¹⁴ And it came to pass, that, when Abram was come into Egypt, the Egyptians beheld the woman that she was very fair. ¹⁵ The princes also of Pharaoh saw her, and commended her before Pharaoh: and the woman was taken into Pharaoh's house. ¹⁶ And he entreated Abram well for her sake: and he had sheep, and oxen, and he asses, and menservants, and maidservants, and she asses, and camels. ¹⁷ And the Lord plagued Pharaoh and his house with great plagues because of Sarai Abram's wife. ¹⁸ And Pharaoh called Abram and said, What is this that thou hast done unto me? why didst thou not tell me that she was thy wife? ¹⁹ Why saidst thou, She is my sister? so I might have taken her to me to wife: now therefore behold thy wife, take her, and go thy way. ²⁰ And Pharaoh commanded his men concerning him: and they sent him away, and his wife, and all that he had.

Like us, Abraham stumbles in his faith. He could trust God to leave and start a new line of descendants (both natural and spiritual), but he could not trust God to keep him and Sarah safe. He concocted a lie and asked his wife to agree to keep them both. He not only deceived Pharaoh, but he placed the life of Pharaoh in peril. But for the direct intervention of The Almighty, Abraham could have possibly had blood on his hands. God somehow communicated supernaturally with Pharaoh the truth about Sarah and Pharaoh became furious with Abraham.

May I interject here that one would think it highly far-fetched to believe Sarah's beauty is that captivating. Reading this chapter for the first time, one would have thought that Abraham had some serious psychological issue. Major paranoia! Abraham's first instinct concerning the selfish and homicidal heart of Pharaoh as nothing but sinister was correct. Who kills a man because he is so enamored with his wife's beauty only to place her in a harem of women? That is not just sick. It is utter evil! It's Abraham's worst fear personified. We can certainly criticize Abraham, but it must be in the light of God's Word and not our self-righteousness. We have all compromised something, somewhere, at some time, in some way, because we, too, lacked the ability to trust God with the outcome. It just so happens that God revealed it to Moses for our information and edification.

When Pharaoh thought Sarah to be Abraham's sister, he took her into his house, which communicates that she is now his property. To make up for this egregious action, he blessed Abraham with things.

Genesis 12:16 states, "And he entreated Abram well for her sake: and he had sheep, and oxen, and he asses, and menservants, and maidservants, and she asses, and camels."

Dowries were customary during those times. Pharaoh paying for Sarah's hand in marriage was no big deal. Abraham taking the dowry under false pretenses was a big deal. That was not right. However, after God revealed the truth to Pharaoh, he put Abraham, Sarah, and all of their stuff out with them. I believe this, too, shows the malevolent heart of Pharaoh as he is trying to ease his guilty conscience. Out of sight, out of mind. If he really thought himself the victim, why didn't he ask for or take back the dowry? When Apostle Paul declares that all things work together for the good for those that love the Lord and are called according to His purpose (Romans 8:28), that includes Abraham.

I'm not making light of his lapse in faith. I am not suggesting that we take advantage of the grace of God. I am, however, showing you that you have the same traits as your father, Abraham. You are not precluded from the presence of God, the love of God, the favor of God, nor the blessing of the Lord that makes rich and adds no sorrow

(Proverbs 10:22) because you missed the mark. Although it was terrible moment and blemish on Abraham's record, he left richer. Abraham used his natural wits to deal with a problem only to be cast out, but he is still righteous and rich.

Certainly, we are not celebrating the faults of Abraham, but we do need to address them to gain a better understanding of how God operates.

You would think Abraham has learned that he can trust God. Right? No! The same situation repeats itself: different faces, same results.

Let's look at Genesis 20:

> "¹ And Abraham journeyed from thence toward the south country, and dwelled between Kadesh and Shur, and sojourned in Gerar. ² And Abraham said of Sarah his wife, She is my sister: and Abimelech king of Gerar sent, and took Sarah. ³ But God came to Abimelech in a dream by night, and said to him, Behold, thou art but a dead man, for the woman which thou hast taken; for she is a man's wife. ⁴ But Abimelech had not come near her: and he said, Lord, wilt thou slay also a righteous nation? ⁵ Said he not unto me, She is my sister? and she, even she herself said, He is my brother: in the integrity of my heart and innocency of my hands have I done this. ⁶ And God said unto him in a dream, Yea, I know that thou didst this in the integrity of thy heart; for I also withheld thee from sinning against me: therefore suffered I thee not to

touch her. ⁷ Now therefore restore the man his wife; for he is a prophet, and he shall pray for thee, and thou shalt live: and if thou restore her not, know thou that thou shalt surely die, thou, and all that are thine. ⁸ Therefore Abimelech rose early in the morning, and called all his servants, and told all these things in their ears: and the men were sore afraid. ⁹ Then Abimelech called Abraham, and said unto him, What hast thou done unto us? and what have I offended thee, that thou hast brought on me and on my kingdom a great sin? thou hast done deeds unto me that ought not to be done. ¹⁰ And Abimelech said unto Abraham, What sawest thou, that thou hast done this thing? ¹¹ And Abraham said, Because I thought, Surely the fear of God is not in this place; and they will slay me for my wife's sake. ¹² And yet indeed she is my sister; she is the daughter of my father, but not the daughter of my mother; and she became my wife. ¹³ And it came to pass, when God caused me to wander from my father's house, that I said unto her, This is thy kindness which thou shalt shew unto me; at every place whither we shall come, say of me, He is my brother. ¹⁴ And Abimelech took sheep, and oxen, and menservants, and womenservants, and gave them unto Abraham, and restored him Sarah his wife. ¹⁵ And Abimelech said, Behold, my land is before thee: dwell where it pleaseth thee. ¹⁶ And unto Sarah he said, Behold, I have given thy brother a thousand pieces of silver: behold, he is to thee a covering of the eyes, unto all that are with thee, and with all other: thus she was reproved. ¹⁷ So Abraham prayed unto God: and God healed Abimelech, and his wife, and his maidservants; and they bare children. ¹⁸ For the Lord had fast closed up all the wombs of the house of Abimelech, because of Sarah Abraham's wife."

I cannot say with a pure heart I understand all that is happening here. It is certainly not a model we want to replicate, but we must do our best to see the glory of God as it shines through in the midst of Abraham's weak faith to look for the continued increase of God. Purposely I gave you the entire chapter to read to understand chapter 12 a little better. This lie was a pact that the two of them made on the onset. Sarah is often depicted as some damsel in distress by ministers, but she is okay with the lie. This plan was their strategy for dealing with this issue. This is their go-t. And look, it seems to still work.

Abraham is still not convinced that God is able to keep him in the light of Sarah's beauty. Now King Abimelech is their latest victim and God's pledge to the Covenant is necessary for Abraham's and Sarah's safety and prosperity. God is faithful even when he (Abraham) is unfaithful. This time, although the king is wroth that Abraham would put him and his nation in such a predicament, he is genuinely regretful and seeks to make amends. He throws everything possible at Abraham to thwart the anger of the Lord. This lapse of faith yields Abraham more sheep, oxen, male servants, and female servants. If that were not enough, he gives Abraham 1,000 pieces of silver to compensate Sarah for any distress or embarrassment.

These two passages show the faithfulness of God to His servants, even in disobedience. Abraham becomes richer after a lapse of faith. What? Who does that? You don't know how I hesitated to write parts of this book. But, we must discuss this because self-righteousness is killing the Church. You do not hear of God rebuking Abraham and Sarah for this charade either time. But you do see God being their defense and causing men to be a blessing to them. Increase. We have some learning to do here. We struggle with the blessings of the Lord on a typical day, less known receiving on a bad day. Can I suggest that this is not simply a blessing but also the blessing that makes rich? One would think God would surely be finished with Abraham after the second display of such distrust. No! In the next chapter, God visits Sarah, and Isaac is born.

God never changed His mind about Abraham, nor Sarah, despite their actions. He made them rich and righteous just as He promised them. Jehovah solidified Abraham as the progenitor of the nation with the birth of Isaac. And God rewarded Abraham for being as faithful as he could be in the afterlife by giving him his own territory to house believers until Christ would lead captivity captive – Abraham's Bosom (Luke 16:23; Ephesians 4:8). Isn't this amazing? He was rich and righteous on earth and in the afterlife.

It is apparent that we need to expand our knowledge for it to impact our faith because we do not hear this Word taught to us consequentially and adequately. We are constantly bribing God for wealth or fighting the voices in our minds and in the Body of Christ who say we should be content with righteousness alone. If we lived in a righteous world, maybe so. But because of the evil, rebellion, and pride in the hearts of man, we are in constant need of God's intervention to make things right, even when we are wrong. He is a God of equity. As it relates to this world, God will supply our need according to His riches in glory by Christ Jesus (Philippians 4:19). There is no Scripture that suggests God won't give me more supply than I need. It is well within His purview to make you rich and righteous should He choose to like He did with the forerunners. We have an established pattern. It is time for you to get your pattern size and be a blessing to the Kingdom like your Father Abraham...with all of his flaws.

CHAPTER 4

 # The Ancestry

The revelation of who we are is best encapsulated by Paul in 1 Corinthians 5:17 when he called us "new creatures." Unfortunately, this information is not as revelatory for the Jewish Church as it is for the Gentile Church. From its days of Abraham, Israel had an understanding of God's favor, His partiality for them, and from the days of Egypt, they had a working knowledge of the depths and lengths He would go through for their continued salvation. They have had well over four thousand years, and counting, of history, compared to our meager two thousand years as converted Gentiles. Israel can trace their history back to Abram, while most of us cannot claim a spiritual pedigree, and if we do, it is of a satanic root (witchcraft, sorcery, and divination).

From out of the gate, they could see God's faithfulness to them, financially, by how He blessed Abraham because of his vast wealth, and ultimately from Egypt, economically, when He told them to borrow vessels of gold and silver (Exodus 3:22). He even made a covenant with them that included economic world dominance. He was serious about them having and maintaining economic independence as a people, which translates to them experiencing economic independence on a personal level–the nation cannot thrive if the people are not independently stable themselves.

Deuteronomy 28:12 tells us, "The Lord shall open unto thee his good treasure, the heaven to give the rain unto thy land in his season, and to bless all the work of thine hand: and thou shalt lend unto many nations, and thou shalt not borrow."

God holds the understanding of finance; it is a wisdom that derives from Him–not a class in economics from an Ivy League school. God knows, God endorses, and God celebrates the financial prosperity of His children. The only way you can find out what He has for you is to start working the gifts, talents, and interests He has given you. Any other voice is a lying spirit from the caverns of Hell, trying to keep you enslaved to poverty. It keeps you working to build another man's wealth or keeps you subjugated to the world system to control your success by controlling you financially.

We are unlike this world. We are a People living within the borders of many nations around the world, comprised of different tongues, nationalities, and experiences. God has made promises to us that come from our fore-parents who may not necessarily be in our bloodline. God recognizes them as our parents by the Spirit. This tie you have with them is as strong as those individuals who are born with direct progeny. You must always keep in the forefront of your mind the spiritual dynamics that are associated with the Kingdom of God. We are the Children of God by the Spirit, while Israel's claim of sonship came through their forefathers (Abraham, Isaac, and Jacob). We have become Children of The Covenant by the testament of Jesus Christ, of which the writer declares in Hebrews 8:6, "⁶But now hath he obtained a more excellent ministry, by how much also he is the mediator of a better covenant, which was established upon better promises."

I have heard some preachers suggest that because the Book of Hebrews was not explicitly written for the Gentile audience, it probably should not have been canonized or not focused on by non-Hebrews. I find the entire argument absurd. The writer does a magnificent job articulating to the converted Hebrews that they could feel free to leave the temple and the old testament rituals. The writer emphatically states this new thing God has done is *better* than the old thing they are encouraging them to unembrace.

Who better than a natural Hebrew to walk us through the covenant? God did not leave us an individualized group to start something new and do the best we could. He connected us to a branch that existed before our regeneration, and one that already had His favor and attention.

Romans 11:24 states, "For if thou wert cut out of the olive tree which is wild by nature, and wert grafted contrary to nature into a good olive tree: how much more shall these, which be the natural branches, be grafted into their own olive tree?"

We were that wild branch. We are not being grafted but have been grated for over two thousand years by the death and resurrection of our Lord and Savior Jesus Christ. The purity of the good tree belongs to us, too. Some people in our Lord's Church do not want all the people to have the same access to the same promises and subsequently the same blessings. They would have sectors and vast numbers of the people subordinate to them and dependent on them for their own enterprise and ego – not to mention the well-being of their families. But that is not what the Bible has ordained, which is why I wrote this book to set you free from Christian exploitation and Christian oppression. The longer you don't read your Bible, the longer you don't ask questions, the longer you will stay in the place of feeling frustrated hearing the Word. You will wonder why God has not done certain things in your life that you read being done in the lives of others. Herein lies our problem: Certain leaders want to cherry-pick which Scriptures are applicable today. When I see God blessing you, and you attributing those blessings to Him, but you tell me to be satisfied with what God has done in my life (to be content) – there is a problem. I do not want what you have. I want everything God has for me.

There is a vast difference between coveting and covenant. Merriam-Webster defines covet as to desire (what belongs to another) inordinately or culpably. It is a thirsty lust for something that belongs to someone else, typically coupled with actions that know no bounds to have what is being coveted. We are not lusting for a covenant. How can you lust for what you already have? I don't think we can even label this as a ratifying of the covenant because God has already approved it. There are scales upon the eyes of some of the saints. There is an ignorance of the covenant in the Body of Christ. And others are being taught a false gospel, which is why Jesus said we are to learn of Him (Matthew 11:29). But I am here to enlighten you.

We are the children of covenant. Our covenant is not one predicated on an old one but is fresh, new, and eternal. We are a class of individuals who are dearly beloved by God. Pay close attention here: The ramifications of rejecting His Son are eternally disastrous, but those consequences do not initialize until after death. However, once you receive Christ as your Lord and Savior, your benefits kick in immediately. There's not even a probationary period. Say this out loud: Every promise of the Book is mine; every chapter, verse, and line!

The antecedents of The Faith are paramount to our understanding of God. Not simply who He is but also the boundaries He has set for our lives. We still learn from them. We look to them for the dos and don'ts! Some would like to debate the fact that Israel was a theocracy as if that would present a problem to God. If God lacks the ability to bless me in the midst of a heathenistic society, He should not call Himself God. I would submit Noah to you along with Enoch. Both individuals escaped the judgment of God upon their evil [heathenistic] generation because of their godliness. Where you reside and who you are surrounded by has no power over God's ability to bring wealth into your life. To that end, I want to provide you with a list of biblical characters who were wealthy, very rich, and extremely rich. I will not provide any commentary as you can research them in your personal study time to find out more information about their economic situations.

Isaac

Genesis 26:13-15

"¹³ And the man waxed great, and went forward, and grew until he became very great:

¹⁴ For he had possession of flocks, and possession of herds, and great store of servants: and the Philistines envied him."

Jacob

Genesis 30:43

"⁴³ And the man increased exceedingly, and had much cattle, and maidservants, and menservants, and camels, and asses."

David

1 Chronicles 29: 3-5, 28

"³ Moreover, because I have set my affection to the house of my God, I have of mine own proper good, of gold and silver, which I have given to the house of my God, over and above all that I have prepared for the holy house. ⁴ Even three thousand talents of gold, of the gold of Ophir, and seven thousand talents of refined silver, to overlay the walls of the houses withal: ⁵ The gold for things of gold, and the silver for things of silver, and for all manner of work to be made by the hands of artificers. And who then is willing to consecrate his service this day unto the Lord? ²⁸ And he died in a good old age, full of days, riches, and honour: and Solomon his son reigned in his stead."

Leaders Of The People

1 Chronicles 29:6-9

"⁶ Then the chief of the fathers and princes of the tribes of Israel and the captains of thousands and of hundreds, with the rulers of the king's work, offered willingly, ⁷ And gave for the service of the house of God of gold five thousand talents and ten thousand drams, and of silver ten thousand talents, and of brass eighteen thousand talents, and one hundred thousand talents of iron. ⁸ And they with whom precious stones were found gave them to the treasure of the house of the Lord, by the hand of Jehiel the Gershonite. ⁹ Then the people rejoiced, for that they offered willingly, because with perfect heart they offered willingly to the Lord: and David the king also rejoiced with great joy."

Solomon

2 Chronicles 9:13-28

"¹³ Now the weight of gold that came to Solomon in one year was six hundred and threescore and six talents of gold; ¹⁴ Beside that which chapmen and merchants brought. And all the kings of Arabia and governors of the country brought gold and silver to Solomon. ¹⁵ And king Solomon made two hundred targets of beaten gold: six hundred shekels of beaten gold went to one target. ¹⁶ And three hundred shields made he of beaten gold: three hundred shekels of gold went to one shield. And the king put them in the house of the forest of Lebanon. ¹⁷ Moreover the king made a great throne of ivory, and overlaid it with pure gold. ¹⁸ And there were six steps to the throne, with a footstool of gold, which were fastened to the throne, and stays on each side of the sitting place, and two lions standing by the stays: [19] And twelve lions stood there on the one side and on the other upon the six steps. There was not the like made in any kingdom. [20] And all the drinking vessels of king Solomon were of gold, and all the vessels of the house of the forest of Lebanon were of pure gold: none were of silver; it was not any thing accounted of in the days of Solomon. [21] For the king's ships went to Tarshish with the servants of Huram: every three years once came the ships of Tarshish bringing gold, and silver, ivory, and apes, and peacocks. [22] And king Solomon passed all the kings of the earth in riches and wisdom. [23] And all the kings of the earth sought the presence of Solomon, to hear his wisdom, that God had put in his heart. [24] And they brought every man his present, vessels of silver, and vessels of gold, and raiment, harness, and spices, horses, and mules, a rate year by year. [25] And Solomon had four thousand stalls for horses and chariots, and twelve thousand horsemen; whom he bestowed in the chariot cities, and with the king at Jerusalem. [26] And he reigned over all the kings from the river even unto the land of the Philistines, and to the border of Egypt. [27] And the king made silver in Jerusalem as stones, and cedar trees made he as the sycomore trees that are in the low plains in abundance. [28] And they brought unto Solomon horses out of Egypt, and out of all lands."

Hezekiah

2 Chronicles 32:26-28

"[26] Notwithstanding Hezekiah humbled himself for the pride of his heart, both he and the inhabitants of Jerusalem, so that the wrath of the Lord came not upon them in the days of Hezekiah. ²⁷ And Hezekiah had exceeding much riches and honour: and he made himself treasuries for silver, and for gold, and for precious stones, and for spices, and for shields, and for all manner of pleasant jewels; ²⁸ Storehouses also for the increase of corn, and wine, and oil; and stalls for all manner of beasts, and cotes for flocks.

Joseph Of Arimathea

Matthew 27:56

"⁵⁶ Among which was Mary Magdalene, and Mary the mother of James and Joses, and the mother of Zebedees children.

"⁵⁷ When the even was come, there came a rich man of Arimathaea, named Joseph, who also himself was Jesus' disciple:

Mark 15:42, 44

"⁴² And now when the even was come, because it was the preparation, that is, the day before the sabbath, ⁴³ Joseph of Arimathaea, an honourable counsellor, which also waited for the kingdom of God, came, and went in boldly unto Pilate, and craved the body of Jesus.

Luke 23:50, 51

"⁵⁰And, behold, there was a man named Joseph, a counsellor; and he was a good man, and a just: ⁵¹ (The same had not consented to the counsel and deed of them;) he was of Arimathaea, a city of the Jews: who also himself waited for the kingdom of God.

Centurion Soldier

Luke 7:1-10

"¹ Now when he had ended all his sayings in the audience of the people, he entered into Capernaum. ² And a certain centurion's servant, who was dear unto him, was sick, and ready to die. 3 And when he heard of Jesus, he sent unto him the elders of the Jews, beseeching him that he would come and heal his servant. ⁴ And when they came to Jesus, they besought him instantly, saying, That he was worthy for whom he should do this: ⁵ For he loveth our nation, and he hath built us a synagogue. ⁶ Then Jesus went with them. And when he was now not far from the house, the centurion sent friends to him, saying unto him, Lord, trouble not thyself: for I am not worthy that thou shouldest enter under my roof: ⁷ Wherefore neither thought I myself worthy to come unto thee: but say in a word, and my servant shall be healed. ⁸ For I also am a man set under authority, having under me soldiers, and I say unto one, Go, and he goeth; and to another, Come, and he cometh; and to my servant, Do this, and he doeth it. ⁹ When Jesus heard these things, he marvelled at him, and turned him about, and said unto the people that followed him, I say unto you, I have not found so great faith, no, not in Israel. ¹⁰ And they that were sent, returning to the house, found the servant whole that had been sick."

Cornelius

Acts 10:1-4

"¹ There was a certain man in Caesarea called Cornelius, a centurion of the band called the Italian band, ² A devout man, and one that feared God with all his house, which gave much alms to the people, and prayed to God alway. ³ He saw in a vision evidently about the ninth hour of the day an angel of God coming in to him, and saying unto him, Cornelius. ⁴ And when he looked on him, he was afraid, and said, What is it, Lord? And he said unto him, Thy prayers and thine alms are come up for a memorial before God.

We have biblical record, both from the Old Testament and the New Testament, of individuals who were able to navigate their Faith and their wealth. Even some of which the Scripture conveys their wealth coming solely from the actions of God. There is nothing left to be said about the plausibility of being righteous and being rich. Henceforth we will now begin to look at the physical and spiritual dynamics that go along with this type of wealth to lay a foundation of realistic expectation of God [from Him of us and from us of Him].

CHAPTER 5

Righteous Trouble

If you think being righteously rich is the end of trouble, you will be an extremely disappointed Christian. *You should expect trouble.* Your prayers will not be answered any faster (no direct line to the Throne of God), there is no additional power to resist Satan, and everybody will not love you. Becoming a believer was not the end of trouble, and neither will being righteous and rich.

On a natural level, you must contend with people who only want your money, not you and others who are envious of your success. This is where those long-term friendships find their importance. Even with the spiritual gift of discerning spirits (1 Corinthians 12:10), you can still let down your guards only to find out you have nurtured a snake. You must also pay close attention to those people who have been around you for a while. It is possible, you may not have actually seen their true heart yet.

Psalm 41:9 states, "Yea, mine own familiar friend, in whom I trusted, which did eat of my bread, hath lifted up his heel against me."

No one but God really knows what lurks in the hearts of people. That goes for the heart of your family, too. Trouble will come in all shapes and sizes. Naturally and spiritually.

On a spiritual level, the powers of darkness will probably create a new dossier on you because you are now a different type of threat to its kingdom. You are now an enabler, a person who has the power to affect the abilities and outcomes of others. As long as you were struggling, you were a different classification of believer, someone hoping and praying. The manifestation of wealth has to draw the attention of Hell because of your righteous affection for God. *Satan has a supreme intellect.* He is no fool. He knows what you will do with the wealth that is now in your power. It's called good works on steroids. You will now be under constant surveillance and periodic attacks that will try to both weaken your love of God and subtracting from your wealth. To say you must be vigilant is an understatement. I am not trying to open a door for a spirit of paranoia to access. I am simply stating a biblical fact:

1 Peter 5:8, 9 tells us, "⁸ Be sober, be vigilant; because your adversary the devil, as a roaring lion, walketh about, seeking whom he may devour: ⁹ Whom resist stedfast in the faith, knowing that the same afflictions are accomplished in your brethren that are in the world."

BLESSINGS WITH PERSECUTION

Some Christian leaders have deprived many believers of blessings in this world by associating money and material wealth with worldliness. To add insult to injury, the world piles on to point out any perceived opulence as hypocrisy. Need I remind you; the world does not know Him. And it seems as though some of us in the Church does not either. Pleasure is not intrinsically evil; it is all predicated upon the source of the pleasure, its originator. The world is known for its pleasures, so too is the Kingdom of God. If Satan is the source of the pleasure, then yes, absolutely no good will come from it; however, if God is the source, it will provide you with joy.

Jesus did not preach Christianity. Jesus preached the Kingdom of God. He preached about an invisible realm that has the power to collect specific people to itself. Then He delivered those individuals from the power of sin, protected them from an invisible adversary, supplied their need, endowed them with supernatural power, brought increase into their lives, and then provided them with eternal life when they die. That is what Jesus preached. Being a citizen in the Commonwealth of God affords us all of the benefits of citizenship.

Apostle John, in Revelation 21, tells of a picturesque breathtaking magnificent landscape of the New Jerusalem: The massive City of God, perfectly pitched on four corners suspended above the earth for all eternity. His perfect vision is intertwined with unfathomable details of features that are nonexistent in any historical or current human civilization, such as the provision of light for the entire city with no generating apparatus. Jesus, Himself, will light the whole City (Revelation 21:23). Isn't that amazing? Whatever you want to call it (a city, a continent, a planet), it is the eternal home and reward of those whose names are in the Lamb's Book of Life. However, according to the Word of God, He does not wait until then to bless us. While there are no earthly blessings that can compare to the glory that shall be revealed, there are blessings for us in this present age. And, no human being has the power to decide how the Sovereign God Jehovah blesses you.

In Mark 10:29, 30, we read, "[29] And Jesus answered and said, Verily I say unto you, There is no man that hath left house, or brethren, or sisters, or father, or mother, or wife, or children, or lands, for my sake, and the gospel's, [30] But he shall receive an hundredfold now in this time, houses, and brethren, and sisters, and mothers, and children, and lands, with persecutions; and in the world to come eternal life."

Some commentaries interpret this passage as spiritual things, rewards after this life, or they seek to water down or nullify houses and lands because of the relationships mentioned (brothers, sisters, mother, and children). There is a subjective attitude of limiting the response of what God will do. I struggle with the concept of spiritual persecutions; even if they derive from the spirit realm, they register on our physical plain, don't they? Is it possible that Jesus can do exceedingly, abundantly above all that we can ask or think?

If He can increase us spiritually, can He also increase us physically? After all, Jesus needed that righteous-rich-disciple, Joseph of Arimathea, to use his influence and wealth to plead for His body (for the resurrection).

Well, it is caveat time. We are now ready to start the process of separating the men from the boys and the women from the girls. There is nothing wrong with boys and girls as long as they stay in their assigned places. The maturity that is required for receiving the great blessings from the Lord is clearly delineated here by Jesus. Frequently, believers want the great blessings of the Lord, but their faith does not qualify them.

Caveat! Verse 30 sounds exciting. Does it not? But do you have what it takes to receive those types of blessings? Oh, sure, we want them, but they cost considerably. Most believers don't like what is prescribed here; suffer then receive. Or they are fearful (or ignorant) of blessings, therefore they preach and teach to suffer now and receive later. Newsflash: you are going to suffer regardless of your beliefs or preferences.

John 16:33 tells us, "These things I have spoken unto you, that in me ye might have peace. In the world ye shall have tribulation: but be of good cheer; I have overcome the world."

Beware of teachings that contradict the Word of God. If you have no problems in your life, you have no place to qualify you for great blessings. When I was a kid in church, I heard the preacher talk about common grace; the type of blessings that even unbelievers receive, e.g., waking up in the morning, life, health, strength, etc. But as a believer, you need that grace that causes you to qualify when you should be disqualified.

I do not understand how Christians can hold the sins of others against them (especially while they still sin themselves). You are a child of God. Your life story should be filled with comebacks and triumphs. There is something evil in a person's heart when you seek to oppress others and not liberate others. Jesus came that you might have an abundant life in the present age and eternal life in the world to come. The only people upset about that message of Christ are Satanists, and sadly they are peppered throughout the Church and they spew their evil toxin every chance they get. My issue with the so-called gospel of prosperity is its slight to holiness and sanctification. It gives the appearance of people practicing spiritual laws of giving instead of practicing their faith in Jesus Christ; loving your neighbor, praying for your enemies, picking up your cross, turning the other cheek, forgiveness, etc. It seems Jesus is mentioned as an almost footnote to get the riches but not the righteousness, when for a fact, it's the life lived for Christ that is all-encompassing. All things still come of thee, Oh Lord! The slightest drift toward the things could possibly end in a diminishing of things. Jesus said if we seek the Kingdom and its righteousness, things would be added. It only stands to reasons if we drift from that righteousness things can be taken away.

During times of trouble, we get an opportunity, and others get a chance to see what lurks in our hearts. Will we hold on to the integrity of the Word, or will we throw caution to the wind and look for any possible way to move the trouble? Or worse, will you get angry with God and feel He is unjust in His treatment towards you?

No believer is exempt from trouble. Jesus reveals to us in Mark 10:29-30 how God operates. When we make sacrifices for His Kingdom, God will reward us greatly in this world. Many believers have the proper understanding and heart when it comes to trouble, but the wrong expectation about the trouble. After we have correctly gone through the trouble, God chooses the reward and the magnitude of it, and still, He gives us eternal life. Therefore, when problems come, execute the Word and watch God bring the increase.

As long as you hold on to the lie of wealth being innately evil or suffer on earth and reward in Heaven, you reject the blessing plan of the Lord. His plan comes to you in this world to prematurely reward you for service well done. How many Christian generations have missed this while living in poverty? And how have other Christians prevented many Christian generations from receiving because of their oppressive nature?

People with an oppressive nature like to rule people or feel entitled to rule over people. They are persecutors. Through them persecution comes. Listen closely because here is where believers miss it. More than not, believers become highly disenchanted with God during times of persecution—because of the perceived unfairness—but they don't stay around long enough to experience the exaltation above their enemies. Saints are notorious for throwing in the towel or withdrawing. The Bible does not teach of victory that resembles giving up or shrinking in position. You must have the mindset of an overcomer.

Revelation 21:7 states, "He that overcometh shall inherit all things; and I will be his God, and he shall be my son."

We read Scripture from a historical aspect and do our best to try and ascertain the thought processes of characters we read about. Unless the Scripture speaks of that mindset specifically, there is no way to know what was going on in their minds and what are the true intentions of God. Case in point: we read of the persecutions of the early Church and ascribe them as overcomers because of their martyrdom. I am not saying that is wrong, but I want to submit to you that something else could happen. I was not there, therefore I cannot say they gave up, but when Peter was in prison, the Church prayed, and an angel released Peter from his cell. Peter showed up at the house where the saints were praying, and after knocking on the door and announcing himself, he still had trouble getting in the house (Acts 12:1-16).

Do you get my point? I can't speak directly to the mindset of the young lady who answered the door other than the Word, that said she was overjoyed, but an argument can be made concerning her expectation of the prayer meeting and the others. Why were they praying if they did not expect God to move? Could it be they were only praying for Peter's strength as he went through a horrible time, and they simply didn't know that angels could be deployed of the Father to release Peter? I don't know, but I can say unequivocally that believers do not always have the faith for God to do His form of overcoming. If we can't conceive a big picture that ends with deliverance, at least we should pray for Him to "do" above and beyond all that we can ask or think (Ephesians 3:20). Dying is all right because to die is gain, but what about seeing His goodness in the land of the living (Psalm 23:17)? No more should we assume trouble means the end. Release your faith and ask God to make you an overcomer. That way you can inherit all things that have been designated for you in this world and the world to come. A part of overcoming is God elevating you to a place of favor that causes those who have worked against you to come to the revelation themselves that you are a child of God.

Revelation 3:9 King James Version states, "Behold, I will make them of the synagogue of Satan, which say they are Jews, and are not, but do lie; behold, I will make them to come and worship before thy feet, and to know that I have loved thee."

For this to happen, we must have an overcomer's attitude. If these satanic individuals are paying homage after being forced to do so, what were they doing before? Remember, if Satan is involved, there is always stealing, killing, and destruction (St. John 10:10a). Trouble always infers some type of demonic power being exercised over a believer, but according to God's Word, He will not allow this to continue perpetually. Even Peter said He would come after we have suffered a while to establish us (1 Peter 5:10). You must set your goal to make it to the other side of the trouble where there is lifting and blessings for you. Also, through the manifestation of Scripture, people come to the revelation of the Word and the knowledge of Christ. It witnesses to both believers and unbelievers. For the sake of the millions of believers who are unrealized, due to the pre-Apollos-like teachings they sit under, we must pursue the promises of God to allow our testimonies to awaken them, regardless of the verbal assaults and attacks we experience because of the truth about righteousness and riches. In the first part of the verse, Jesus says, "I will make." You should remain humble and focus on the work He has called you to and let Him take care of the rest. Let Him take care of your detractors, while you keep working for The Kingdom.

The Word tells us to ask for wisdom if we realize it is absent in our lives (James 1:5). The importance of having a level of wisdom is the degree of comfort and confidence it provides. Knowing the truths of God cannot be over-emphasized. Far too many believers stress themselves needlessly because they refuse to read and familiarize themselves with the Word of God. Others reject the comfort of Holy Spirit when He tries to reassure them during times of trouble. Giving your life to the Lord in no way is an exemption from trouble, actually, it is the opposite. Only when you have moved from labor to reward are you free from trouble. There is a comfort in knowing that the same way He was with you in lack, He will be with you in plenty. You will have enemies, but they will flee from you seven ways (Deuteronomy 28:7). Yes, trouble will come. Temptations will come. Even sorrow will come. But we are overcomers.

CHAPTER 6

Un-Righteous Rich: Bad Practices

Psalm 62:10 gives this advice: "If riches increase, set not your heart on them." The insight provided by the Word of God coupled with the constant companionship of Holy Ghost is invaluable to us as believers. God watches over His Word to perform it is not only a Scripture we quote, but it is a hook we can hang our hats on. Should we forget about the luxury this promise provides, we have His Spirit to remind us, that way we will not suffer the possibility of going astray emotionally. There are books contained in the Bible that can definitely give us a competitive edge over our secular competition. And those same books will share devastating pitfalls to look out for as you do business and handle money. Nothing comes easy, and nothing remains easy. The same work it took to develop a character that pleases God enough to place wealth in your hands, will require the same fortitude to maintain it in a godly manner.

I want to share a few of these pitfalls with you. These pitfalls are easily descended into by believers and can be extremely difficult to get out of quickly. I genuinely believe many of you are reading this book by a divine purpose. You have suffered a while, and now He has come to establish you (1 Peter 5:10). I believe suffering taught you to appreciate the statues of God, even as the Psalmist in 119 articulated. Learning to live within the statues of God requires discipline that is contrary to the world, and sadly, contrary to too many believers today. Having the ability to go out of the plan of God to fulfill one's desire or need is easy, having the discipline to deny your flesh to wait on God is not so easy.

I believe many of you have developed such a discipline, or you now understand what God has been doing in your life over the past years. He was not denying you but rather developing you for a righteous rich life. The first test is also the recurring theme for all righteous and rich believers: Can you handle access to the wealth and at the same time not use it if you are instructed not to do so? This is the first level of discipline you will need being a victorious righteous and rich believer. More on this in a moment.

Just as the Word has provided righteous and rich people for us to pattern our lives after, there are unrighteous and rich people whose behaviors we need to highlight, talk about, and mark as unprofitable. No matter how wealthy or poor we are, all of us are on a mission not to be an unprofitable servant of our God. I am sure you will probably think of some others mentioned in Scripture and even some contemporaries who could make the list. Find whatever information and inspiration you need to help you to remain a profitable servant!

The grace and mercy of God is strange. It will open a door for you even with the knowledge of your inability to manage the success on the other side. It will lift you, knowing you cannot handle what comes with exaltation. You better know what you are getting yourself into when it comes to being righteous and rich. Success must be managed. For many of you, this is why God humbled you before blessing you. It is not easy; it takes work to keep your flesh under subjection. Do not be like King Saul.

1 Samuel 15:16-18 states, "[16] Then Samuel said unto Saul, Stay, and I will tell thee what the Lord hath said to me this night. And he said unto him, Say on. [17] And Samuel said, When thou wast little in thine own sight, wast thou not made the head of the tribes of Israel, and the Lord anointed thee king over Israel?"

The Scripture gives no indication of Saul asking to become king by the will of God or his own volition. God still expected that he would rise to the occasion. The prophet Samuel said there was a time when King Saul was humbled about himself and his appointment, which made him the right choice for the position, but he became arrogant, disobedient, and stubborn over the course of time. He forgot his humbled beginnings as king and started to throw his weight around, even towards God Almighty – mistake.

It is your job to keep yourself surrounded by people who will tell you the truth about yourself and not placate you because they are on the payroll; they were taught to regard your feelings, or are afraid of you. You owe it to yourself, to your family, to God, to the Church, to do everything within your power to keep yourself as a humble servant before the Lord. If not, do not find yourself surprised when God comes to expose you before everyone, or worst, He strips you of everything.

DO NOT FORGET GOD

The children of Israel were warned by God, Himself, about the dangers of forgetting Him and the proclivities they had to do such a thing. We must remember that in the flesh, there dwells no good thing. Period! You cannot reform your flesh. It is inherently deceitful and inherently evil. We cannot place any confidence in it.

Deuteronomy 6:10-12 states, "[10] And it shall be, when the Lord thy God shall have brought thee into the land which he sware unto thy fathers, to Abraham, to Isaac, and to Jacob, to give thee great and goodly cities, which thou buildedst not, [11] And houses full of all good things, which thou filledst not, and wells digged, which thou diggedst not, vineyards and olive trees, which thou plantedst not; when thou shalt have eaten and be full; [12] Then beware lest thou forget the Lord, which brought thee forth out of the land of Egypt, from the house of bondage."

Is not that just like The Father to point out the exact place we need to set a watch? Success is not an easy thing to manage. As you read, He told them the dangers that come thereafter. One of the definitions for "forget" in the Hebrew is "to cease to care about." Wow! Come on. How can you "cease to care about" the One solely responsible for you being in the position? Israel did that. Don't say, "I would never forget the Lord." Israel was comprised of people like us. Material possessions got too easy for them to acquire. God was no longer needed for daily bread, therefore He became a non-entity to them.

The system He created for them worked perfectly. They thought it was their power that worked the system. On the contrary, it was God and God alone. If you don't believe me, answer this question: Why could they do nothing about the consequences of "ceasing to care about" Him? Why did the ground cease to yield its fruit to them? Why did the protection from their enemies cease? They stopped caring, and God ceased providing. Don't forget the Lord.

ENTITLEMENT

Be sober in your thinking and interactions with God. While we are all His children, He does not play favorites. All of us are assigned positions and tasks based upon our abilities He has given to us (St. Matthew 25:15). One of the worst assumptions to make is that you have the hook-up with God. He is not your inside man. You, too, are required to be where you should be, doing what you should be doing. Too many people have a sense of entitlement in the natural, and now it has seeped into the Church. But, this is what the Word says about how we should handle our giftedness.

Ecclesiastes 9:11 tells us, "I returned, and saw under the sun, that the race is not to the swift, nor the battle to the strong, neither yet bread to the wise, nor yet riches to men of understanding, nor yet favour to men of skill; but time and chance happeneth to them all."

Just because you are anointed, had a dream, were given a prophetic word, are extremely intelligent, have the next great invention, etc., does not mean you are guaranteed success. The writer said after his many observations, he deduced that we must be willing to deal with the ebbs and flows of life and markets as well as our ability to finish.

It might work today, and it might not work next week. Acting like spoiled babies will not hasten the solution. Expecting things always to be easy is immature and demanding that God responds when you want Him to respond is a no-go.

Prayer is coupled with faith, and faith is coupled with work. You are not entitled to success. Always remain gracious and humbled before God no matter what, as you pursue your Kingdom assignments with all of your strength.

PURSUING WEALTH

The goal is not to become rich but rather to be a living conduit for the Kingdom of Heaven to channel money, power, and influence to and through you. The pipes in your home have no other purpose than preparing the valves for release. The pipes do not look for water. They channeled what is supplied. Keep this analogy in mind and it will help you to avoid the pitfall of chasing money. Character, ethics, integrity are all essential to us. It may be an easy investment or market, but that does not mean you should be associated with it. The standard of who and what we seek has been established by the Great Head of The Church. It is cemented and it never changes. It remains the same regardless of the economic climate we find ourselves, be it good or poor. Our purpose of living is only for Jesus Christ. We read in Proverbs 23:4, "Labour not to be rich: cease from thine own wisdom."

Desperation and opportunity are two culprits you must beware of as Satan will use them to draw you off path. They are two of the many mirages he presents to us as a seemingly legitimate excuses for pursuing wealth. You must have the power as a righteous and rich believer to reject a winning proposal because you already have enough money. You must also be strong enough when you hit a down market to seek the will of God concerning your next step, and not allow people to pressure you into making unethical decisions that impugn your character, and your reputation for a quick return. Remember Job's response when he lost everything. That is how you want to be. Trust God with money in the bank and trust Him when the account is low! I saw the title of a movie, "Get Rich, or Die Trying," and immediately knew that wasn't a Kingdom philosophy but the manifest difference between the world and the Church. Do not overwhelm yourself with getting rich; righteousness is always our primary focus, and He will add everything else (Matthew 6:33).

PRIDE

The word pride suggests there is an exaggerated opinion of self-importance; a personal sense that the sun revolves around you. Along with this attitude comes a host of behaviors that will lead you to ruins if you do not crucify your flesh. Two behaviors we find are self-sabotaging: *self-governance and abuse of people*. Pride will always tell me, "that does not apply to me." If I find it easy to break the law of the land, it will become just as easy to break the Law of Christ. Having money is powerful. Power must be managed, or we run the risk of thinking we can match power to power with the All-Mighty. Pride alters your thinking. You know better, but you find yourself doing what you would not normally do because your thinking has been corrupted. While pride is natural for the flesh, it is abnormal for the spirit. According to the Word of God, acknowledging and fighting this contradiction will elicit a response from God.

Proverbs 22:4 states, "The reward for humility is fear of Adonai, along with wealth, honor and life" (Complete Jewish Bible).

Dialing down the self-image to the degree that God recognizes it has humility (a dependence on Him for all things) will accelerate the Lord's blessings in your life. In contrast, pride will cause Him to move His hand of protection from you, leaving you open prey for the powers of darkness.

LOVING MONEY

Most believers are extremists. They live carefully as not to do anything that could, in their minds, jeopardize their eternal reward. While I do agree with that, we cannot misconstrue the Scripture to fit our narrow belief systems. We must be strong enough to filter our fears through the Word of God and not let our fears change the Word of God but rather challenge us. The Power of God is able to keep us in all of the places He has ordained us to be. You should not fear money because you see how corrupted people chose money over God, money over righteousness. The Scripture is clear about our affections that they should be toward God and God alone. Nothing, and nobody, should infringe on that place where God reigns supreme in our lives. You should view riches, wealth, and money as tools or instruments to help you achieve your earthly goals, laying up more treasure in Heaven where the corruptors cannot access (Matthew 5:19-21).

1 Timothy 6:10 tells us, "For the love of money is the root of all evil: which while some coveted after, they have erred from the faith, and pierced themselves through with many sorrows."

This verse does not speak of unbelievers but saints. Some believers cannot control their lust for money: more is never enough. The word coveted suggests removing God as one's primary desire and replacing Him with money. It also means placing oneself physically in a precarious position by stretching for something to the degree of possibly falling. Need I say more? This is why we do not forsake the teaching of Jesus and His example of living. If we would love God with all of our being, there would not be room for anything else (Deuteronomy 11:13).

CONCLUSION:

These were but a few of the bad practices that could land you in a terrible fix with God. I would, however, underscore the word *practice* to you. The truth is that at our best, we are still filthy rags before a Holy God, but our redeeming quality is our refusal to practice (regular reoccurrences) those behaviors that would break the heart of God. It has even been said that practice makes perfect. The more we highlight the character of God and seek to make His character the light of our lives, the more of His pleasure we will receive. We make choices every day concerning whom we will serve and whose light we will let shine through us. Having money but ignoring spiritual integrity could cause open rebuke and open shame. If we suffer, the apostle Peter said it should because right choices are being made and not because of bad decisions (1 Peter 3:17). Let us endeavor to implement good sound judgment that becomes good practices and not bad choices that lead to bad practices.

CHAPTER 7

No More Reproach

The word reproach means to find fault with (a person, group, organization, etc.); blame; censure. There has been enough criticism levied at the Church and justly so. When the world's criticism of the Church is correct, you know we have a problem. While some pastors and leaders may have welcomed this book, here is where we must self-correct to rise above the scrutiny of the world as they continue to look for church hypocrisy. We may not be able to fix all of it, but at least we can look them back in their eyes and point to where it works and not hang our heads in shame because they are right. The world should not want our Christ because of an authentic rejection of Him, not because we have dropped the ball somewhere and refuse to address our integrity, character, or perception.

Over the years, the Church has gotten a bad reputation for amalgamating Church and business to the degree that money looks like the objective and not Jesus for the people. Please do not think that I am naive when I stress that we should not use the Church as our primary source for the enterprise because there are financial transactions that should take place according to the Word of God. Here is one:

1 Corinthians 9:11-14 we read, "¹¹ If we have sown unto you spiritual things, is it a great thing if we shall reap your carnal things? ¹² If others be partakers x this power over you, are not we rather? Nevertheless we have not used this power; but suffer all things, lest we should hinder the gospel of Christ. ¹³ Do ye not know that they which minister about holy things live of the things of the temple? and they which wait at the altar are partakers with the altar? ¹⁴ Even so hath the Lord ordained that they which preach the gospel should live of the gospel."

There is an owed transaction after the Gospel has been delivered. Paul did not say how large or how small; only that the preacher owes a solid word, and the hearer owes something tangible to the preacher.

Here is where it gets dicey for our generation and cause reproach: How much does the hearer owe the preacher? Answer: There is no set amount. You give as the Lord has prospered you, what you will be glad (cheerful) about giving, and you won't hate yourself afterward for giving (2 Corinthians 9:7).

Isn't that simple? No games. No emotional blackmail or prophetic manipulations. Simply share what you're comfortable with giving. The preacher owes it to the people not to live a lifestyle that requires them to break with Scripture, and the people owe it to the preacher to not muzzle the ox that is treading out the corn. That will keep the preacher from growing disenchanted with preaching the Gospel and the people from supporting the Gospel. We are too easily found at fault here, by the world, because we refuse to let Paul's instructions be our guide. Reproach! I used the word dicey to describe the conundrum for our generation regarding these financial transactions associated with Paul's instructions because our generation, like no other, has been blessed financially. During the ministry of Paul, giving something materially could range from a coat, to livestock, to money. In our generation, especially in America, our expectation for the most part is a financial transaction. I am not saying it is correct, simply the foremost drawn conclusion. Now, the danger. Along with our generation being blessed financially, we are also blessed with the gift of technology. And technology is big business.

The Gospel has become big business in our generation. People have found ways of harnessing these technologies and creating juggernauts. Some ministries have amassed literally millions of followers or supporters that give to them financially on a monthly basis. What is the danger? Having such access coupled with a weak character is a recipe for disaster. And we see it all the time. Ministers who began small, with seemingly a pure heart of God and the things of God, are eventually corrupted by the lusts of this world because money, power, and fame gave them access to what they were not capable of managing. As you read this book and possibly find that it liberates you from the mental prison of lack you have been confined to, look at this passage: Proverbs 30:8-10. "⁸ Remove far from me vanity and lies: give me neither poverty nor riches; feed me with food convenient for me: ⁹ Lest I be full, and deny thee, and say, Who is the Lord? or lest I be poor, and steal, and take the name of my God in vain."

As wisdom is still the principal thing, it behooves all of us to ask God to set the boundaries of our lives. That way we will not set ourselves up for temptation we cannot bear. The writer of Proverbs 30 is a gentleman by the name of Agur. He was clear in his request to God, having observed the traps and pitfalls of both the poor and the rich. He deduced for his life, that it would be better for God to prescribe him with the portion of food he needs because if the pendulum of his life swung in either direction too liberally, he would most likely effect his devotion to God.

When I was young, I found out political science was a thing. It was hard for me to wrap my brain around the fact that one could take analysis then manufacture that behavior to the point of manipulations and outcomes. When we see the Church today, we can reasonably say there is a such thing as "church-science."

Do you realize how horrible that is to say? Did you get a knot in your stomach after reading that? I did when I wrote it. There is a group of people who teach, preach, and minister in the Body of Christ who study the current behaviors of the people of God and manufacture sermons, music, and Christian service based on those trends, focus groups, and polls. It is not for the benefit of the hearer, but their own personal enterprise. Damnable evil is what it is. Our finite minds could never produce nor maintain a move of God. And the arrogance in thinking that one knows the mind of God absent of divine communications of the Holy Ghost is the epitome of Satanism. But that is what we have.

Creating these juggernauts and giving no thought to the repercussion of such success is selfish and myopic. The lesson from Agur is: What if I fall? When is the last time you thought about your success in that light? Some people badly want popularity and success, but they never think about the downside. The bubble is not the downside. What if you fall? The Kingdom of God has experienced reproach before, and it will again. But why does it have to be you? Why does it have to be me? We must be astute enough or spiritually sensitive enough to cap our success. There is absolutely nothing wrong with asking God to monitor our going in and going out, our uprising, and our downsitting. We should want to live a life free from scandal, free from reproach.

Agur makes a basic observation regarding having too much; the temptation of forgetting God and pride. But there is a remarkable observation that he makes regarding a consistently poor person or being thrust into poverty. He was astute enough not to judge the person who stole because they fell on hard times and laid that person's lot at the feet of God. We often deduce that a person's heart must be in the wrong place when they do something terrible. Christians are notorious for being black and white thinkers, and hesitant to find out the backstories of people who have offended us or someone we love. In his manifold wisdom, Agur presents this as a problem for God in that this person would be a reproach against God because of this forced behavior. The thief was not depraved, but stole as a desperate measure to survive. Agur clearly states no matter what may befall him, he would never stop loving

God. Even if he had to steal to eat, it would simply be a reproach that God would have to live with.

I saw a story on the news about a man who robbed a store with a baseball bat. The store owner asked why he was doing such a thing, and the robber's reply was to provide for his family that was in need. The store owner told the man he understood, and in lieu of calling the police, the store owner helped the man with $40 and a loaf of bread. The store owner went into the back of the store to get the man some milk, but the man bolted from the store.

A few months later, the owner received a letter of explanation, thanks, apology, and a $50 bill from the would-be robber. I am certainly not encouraging anyone to take such drastic measures because you may not have the same miraculous outcome of compassion. But when people are desperate for the basics of life, they do desperate things, and for the believer, God is still faithful. He can live with the reproach. Bless His Holy Name!

But why is there a need for reproach? There are many questions to be asked in this situation. Did the man lose his job? Why didn't he have savings? Were there any educational disabilities or neglects that contributed to his problem? All of those are good questions and we all need to be accountable. How about this: Was he oppressed or limited by a religious system that shares a bed with a carnal social system that works in tandem to prevent people's success by telling them to be satisfied with what they have, even when what they have is not enough?

Primarily I have focused on the ministry here, but these same principles and concerns ring true for businessmen and businesswomen. There is a stark difference in how the Kingdom does business and how Babylon does business. God is the Father of all of His children. We must learn to play well together, pray together, and even help one another in business. There is a spirit of Babylon that seeks to become the juggernaut, thereafter, buying out or crushing the competition. This is demonic at its core and a worldly practice. It is Antichrist. Reproach! The Body of Christ does not see other parts of the Body as competitors or enemies.

Even in business, we are still the Body of Christ, and we must continually work to produce unity among the faithful. I am not saying we are not wise in our endeavors, but we do not promote being the last man or woman standing. We are all working to a twofold purpose: support the Body of Christ while simultaneously providing for our families to the fullest measure of our abilities and opportunities; that is, without crushing our brothers and sisters. To crush a family member would be a reproach on the Body, even in business. In ministry and business, our actions should be understood from observation. When an elaborate and laborious explanation is needed to justify our decisions, we could be drifting towards or have entered reproach. We owe it to the Great Head of The Church as well as the members of the Body to do everything in our power to avoid the appearance of impropriety.

I clearly remember the first time I went to the studio. I was young, and surrounded by individuals who were older and had much more experience. I listened to them talk back and forth about the direction they wanted to take in the production of a particular song.

After much discussion, I heard one of them chide the other, and say, "Don't forget the K.I.S.S. Rule." I had no idea what they were referencing, therefore I inquired. They said, "That stands for Keep It Simple, Stupid."

We must employ that principle in ministry as well as business. Much of the Fortune 500 domain is based upon cooked books and formulas that smaller companies cannot use (and neither would you want to use those formulas because they are based upon pseudo projections – lies). The standard of God is let your yea be yea and your nay be nay (Matthew 5:37). We are Kingdom citizens, now. We do not require psychological warfare and math manipulations. We don't have to exaggerate our numbers or play with the truth to get ahead. God is our Father; He will bless us. Less we forget, it was God's idea to incorporate and link His blessings to Israel's obedience to His commandments, bringing increase to the work and production or bringing decrease based on if they were derelict in their devotion to Him.

It is His will for His children to take care of the less fortunate: Romans 15:26 states, "For it hath pleased them of Macedonia and Achaia to make a certain contribution for the poor saints which are at Jerusalem."

Who is "them?" Regular people like you and me who see about the needs of those who are not blessed financially. It does not make us better or them lessor. It is the way we show our devotion to God through Jesus Christ. We will look a little deeper into that passage in a later chapter as we delve into community living, but I need you to see here that it pleases God that we support each other financially as well as economically. Doing this removes reproach from us and gives us a standard that the world and false religions would envy.

In conclusion, we must be willing to guard our reputation, collectively as a Church and individually as a member of it. If we are unfair towards one another (family), we should never expect the world to be open to receiving our Christ. Listening is still a lost art form. The Spirit begs us to stop the monologues and start the dialogues. Let us use all of our power and influence to help build the wealth of brothers and sisters in the Body and not individuals of the world.

CHAPTER 8

 ## The Marketplace

The marketplace is ordained by God, and believers should not run away from it, nor should they think the only way to participate in it is by the world's standards. I wrote this book specifically for Christians who feel inadequate to participate in the marketplace, or feel the marketplace is taboo or unrighteous. They may also deal with generational poverty. Too many believers hang their hats on the miracle-working power of God and are dismissive of, or ignorant of, the systematic method He has created for placing wealth and riches in their hands. Both are ordained and both are needed. The Church must embrace the truth of the marketplace if She will be the provocateur prophesied in the book of Romans regarding the nation of Israel (Romans 11:11). Also, the Word has spoken of our extrication from the world system to receive a more stable life:

Revelation 18:4 states, "And I heard another voice from heaven, saying, Come out of her, my people, that ye be not partakers of her sins, and that ye receive not of her plagues."

Do you see how ordained the marketplace really is? Not only will He bless us to sustain us as an independent market, He also has fixed the outcome. As rich as the world system can make its participants, the Scripture says clearly that He sends plagues upon them that limit their success because of their sins. Sidenote: If there is universal salvation because of the death of Jesus, there would be no repercussion because of their sin. The Scripture articulates the sins of the world affect us in the marketplace. If we are to come out of Babylon as we have been commanded, *it will be required that we have our own marketplace.*

One of the mistakes we make as teachers of the Gospel is when we highlight the number of times a word is used in Scripture; whether it is used 400 times or two times, it is essential. The Scripture is not filled with thousands of references about the marketplace, but it is used enough times and alluded to enough to let us know its importance. Also, it is used in a parable of Jesus, which seals the deal for the New Testament Church. Matthew 20:1-16 reads:

> "[1] For the kingdom of heaven is like unto a man that is an householder, which went out early in the morning to hire labourers into his vineyard. [2] And when he had agreed with the labourers for a penny a day, he sent them into his vineyard. [3] And he went out about the third hour, and saw others standing idle in the marketplace, [4] And said unto them; Go ye also into the vineyard, and whatsoever is right I will give you. And they went their way. [5] Again he went out about the sixth and ninth hour, and did likewise. [6] And about the eleventh hour he went out, and found others standing idle, and saith

unto them, Why stand ye here all the day idle? [7] They say unto him, Because no man hath hired us. He saith unto them, Go ye also into the vineyard; and whatsoever is right, that shall ye receive. [8] So when even was come, the lord of the vineyard saith unto his steward, Call the labourers, and give them their hire, beginning from the last unto the first. [9] And when they came that were hired about the eleventh hour, they received every man a penny. [10] But when the first came, they supposed that they should have received more; and they likewise received every man a penny. [11] And when they had received it, they murmured against the goodman of the house, [12] Saying, These last have wrought but one hour, and thou hast made them equal unto us, which have borne the burden and heat of the day. [13] But he answered one of them, and said, Friend, I do thee no wrong: didst not thou agree with me for a penny? [14] Take that thine is, and go thy way: I will give unto this last, even as unto thee. [15] Is it not lawful for me to do what I will with mine own? Is thine eye evil, because I am good? [16] So the last shall be first, and the first last: for many be called, but few chosen."

Parables are true lifelines for the Church as we must contend with the world, from which we have been saved, and live virtuously representing a Kingdom that we have never lived in before. Parables are not only stories. They are ingenious stupefying eternal principled narratives told by Jesus, filled with life and truth. This parable, with all of its Kingdom principles and secrets, tells us that Jesus endorses buying and selling in the marketplace. Not in the temple, but the marketplace.

There is a biblical precedent of a man of God invoking the spirit of prophecy to erase the debt of the wife and family of a fellow prophet who died, leaving his family in financial peril. 2 Kings 4:1-7 states:

> "[1] Now there cried a certain woman of the wives of the sons of the prophets unto Elisha, saying, Thy servant my husband is dead; and thou knowest that thy servant did fear the Lord: and the creditor is come to take unto him my two sons to be bondmen. [2] And Elisha said unto her, What shall I do for thee? tell me, what hast thou in the house? And she said, Thine handmaid hath not any thing in the house, save a pot of oil. [3] Then he said, Go, borrow thee vessels abroad of all thy neighbours, even empty vessels; borrow not a few. [4] And when thou art come in, thou shalt shut the door upon thee and upon thy sons, and shalt pour out into all those vessels, and thou shalt set aside that which is full. [5] So she went from him, and shut the door upon her and upon her sons, who brought the vessels to her; and she poured out. [6] And it came to pass, when the vessels were full, that she said unto her son, Bring me yet a vessel. And he said unto her, There is not a vessel more. And the oil stayed. [7] Then she came and told the man of God. And he said, Go, sell the oil, and

pay thy debt, and live thou and thy children of the rest."

If this righteous and rich life is going to work for you, it will start with you getting something in your hand. You must have a product or service that God can bless in the marketplace. Elisha also told her that she would be so successful from this venture that she would have the option of retiring for the balance of her days. Amazing. She did not know what the man of God would do, but I wonder if she had any idea of the magnitude in which God would bless her? Not only were her children saved, God increased her financially within a matter of days. She has her children and peace of mind. The lady's trouble was turned into triumph. Her vicissitude was turned into complete victory. We don't have to see this example in every book of the Bible. We only need to see it once to create a paradigm for God to flow through. And if we too are willing and obedient, we shall eat, too (Isaiah 1:19).

The marketplace is where each believer or group of believers gets the opportunity to showcase and present their product or service to the public for consumption. According to the Scripture, this is ordained of God. I don't know if you have ever thought about it, but have you noticed that Covenant He made with Israel spoke more to owners than it did to the employees? In Deuteronomy 28:2-4, 11 we read:

> "[2] And all these blessings shall come on thee, and overtake thee, if thou shalt hearken unto the

voice of the Lord thy God. ³ Blessed shalt thou be in the city, and blessed shalt thou be in the field. ⁴ Blessed shall be the fruit of thy body, and the fruit of thy ground, and the fruit of thy cattle, the increase of thy kine, and the flocks of thy sheep. ¹¹ And the Lord shall make thee plenteous in goods, in the fruit of thy body, and in the fruit of thy cattle, and in the fruit of thy ground, in the land which the Lord sware unto thy fathers to give thee.

The greatest attention is given to the individuals who will take it upon themselves to lord over their lives, and property. There is no mention of the blessing being on the workers. The workers are living at the mercy of the owners. God said He would bless the livestock and crops of those who work what He has provided. What has God given you to merchandise, grow, and provide stability for your family and employment for the community? We cannot forsake the paradigm and then ask God to look over it to bless us anyhow. The enemies of The Faith should be borrowing from us, and we should be loaning to them.

We have two significant issues: Most believers work for someone else, and godly individuals or boards do not lead those corporations. The promise of abundance is predicated upon a righteous covenant. A righteous owner, that is you. It is spiritually unethical to ask Him to bless His enemies in order to bless you. You are whom God loves. You are the bearer of His Spirit in the Earth. He sent His Son to die for you. His promises are to you and not His enemies. What is missing from the equation of your abundance is you in your rightful and God-ordained place:

Deuteronomy 28:13 tell us, "And the Lord shall make thee the head, and not the tail; and thou shalt be above only, and thou shalt not be beneath; if that thou hearken unto the commandments of the Lord thy God, which I command thee this day, to observe and to do them:"

For many of you, I say unequivocally, the reason you have had, and have such a difficult time financially is that He has to "make you" hate where you are to get you to the place and position He has ordained for you as the head of the organization and not as a mere employee. You are the one who should call the shots and develop the strategy.

Deuteronomy 28:1 says, "And it shall come to pass, if thou shalt hearken diligently unto the voice of the Lord thy God, to observe and to do all his commandments which I command thee this day, that the Lord thy God will set thee on high above all nations of the earth:"

CONGLOMERATIONS

We must contend with the world system that exists parallel to the Christian market. It does not mean that the world system is greater than ours, better than ours, or should be abandoned for ours; it only means we need to exist alongside them. It has been said that small business is the engine of economic development. Larger companies try to maintain some type of public affinity for small businesses while still garnering more and more of the market share. You cannot have your cake and eat it, too. You are either with them or against them. The proof is in the pudding: Why are larger companies consolidating? Who do you think that consolidation is for? Are the workers getting raises? No. But the executives are becoming richer. The shareholders are being blessed. What happens to the workers who are laid off due to the acquisition of a company, and there is job duplication? Large corporations have substantial market share, and the new idiom is they must consolidate with their competitors to compete with other larger competing companies. Bigger becomes bigger at the cost of the smaller companies. Some people call it capitalism, and others call it greed. Subsidiaries and divisions of these corporations kill small businesses that do not have the resources to compete, or a relationship with the bank's president or other executives. That is wrong. More concerning are the workers who were laid off after years of faithful employment who now find their skill levels antiquated and wanting.

Mega corporations are not only too big to fail; they are too big to compete with. Once, you could depend on the government to play the antitrust card. Since many of these corporations are donors to their political campaigns and parties, they have a greater kinship for their big donors rather than local business owners, their constituents. Between big businesses and lobbyists, local small businesses don't have a leg to stand on. This consolidation of big business is not God's will as it hinders individuals from their personal visions. According to Scripture, God gives individuals, gifts and talents to subsidize their lifestyles (Romans 12:6-8; 1 Thessalonians 4:11).

CHAPTER 9

Buyers of The Marketplace

There is a major educational marketing campaign we must undertake as christianpreneurs (a Christian business owner). We must educate believers on what happens when they support a Christian business. They need to know who that purchase magnifies, and that it broadens the scope and boundaries of the Kingdom of God.

A seller is nothing without a buyer, and the business' success is predicated upon the sale. The wisdom of God is to give talent to the business owner and a palette to the consumer that runs the gamut of the focus of the business owners. Business is not monolithic but rather a diversity of spectrums encompassing old and current trends, while still growing and recognizing new trends. What are those trends? Trends are needs that the public has, but they may or may not be aware they have a need.

The infinite prudence of God has elected to allow nothing of tangibility to last forever. Things will always break down, wear out, or become antiquated. God plans to keep the market fluid. In a nutshell, this is what secular business is: your ability to find your niche, make the public aware of your presence, and then convince them that you are better than the rest. It can be and is incredibly competitive. Please don't let that statement be a rock in your wagon because your God is greater. You are not doing secular business; you are doing Kingdom Business.

Deuteronomy 28:13 tells us, "¹³And the Lord shall make thee the head, and not the tail; and thou shalt be above only, and thou shalt not be beneath; if that thou hearken unto the commandments of the Lord thy God, which I command thee this day, to observe and to do them: God is not afraid of the secular market! It only exists because He has permitted it to exist. He is still capable of making all grace abound toward you" (2 Corinthians 9:8).

The cream must rise to the top because that is its natural composition. So too with your business; it must take its place above the secular businesses of Babylon because God has set it so. You are doing Kingdom Business. You must see your business as a continuation of the ministry of Jesus, the ministry of reconciliation. Some would incorrectly argue the ministry of reconciliation as the simple spreading of the message that Jesus saves. But I would push back because He said His salvation included an abundant life. You must stop assuming the will of God for everyone and allow Holy Ghost to lead them and guide them to the life He has seen for them in the mind of God (Romans 8:27). The people of God must know their options and understand that the color of their skin, their gender, nor their current social class restricts them from the abundant life Jesus came to give them (Galatians 3:28).

See, for too long, we have evangelized in narrow ways: revivals, street ministry, tracks, home Bible studies, knocking on doors in the community, and TV & radio. While each one of those methods is virtuous and vital, they are not the only methods of God. Nothing beats face to face, one on one time. The assumption we make is that the only people needing salvation are those who frequent those places I just mentioned. There are people in need of the Good News that we will not reach with those practices; some of them live in gated communities where you can't simply knock on the door and ask them if they know Jesus. There are some people whose lifestyles are totally out of reach for a poor and struggling believer. The biggest mistake we can ever make as Christians is thinking that only the poor need Jesus. We must end the social war in The Church. The poor cannot afford to be angry with the well-off and rich, and the well-to-do cannot afford to distance themselves from the poor, praying, church mother. Both need each other and both are the will of God for one another. Your business and its success will open doors for you to share your faith at levels you could never have dreamt.

FAVOR OF GOD

You will need buyers and clients for your business. Along with your determination to provide excellent goods and services, know that God will do His part in helping you become successful. The Father touches hearts and changes minds. We read in Proverbs 21:1, "The king's heart is in the hand of the Lord, as the rivers of water: he turneth it whithersoever he will."

The public's response to your venture is also within the wheelhouse of God (it is His specialty). For you or I to manipulate the mind of a person is forbidden, it is called witchcraft when we do it; however, when God does it, it is His prerogative as Creator. God can require or cause an individual or group of people to do whatever He desires of them. Lest we forget, we were created for His pleasure. Whatever brings joy to Him, He performs. And remember, it is His good pleasure to give us the Kingdom, Jesus said (Luke 12:32). Don't fret about your product or service. Don't fret about your clientele. Don't fret about your business. I'm telling you not to worry, period. God is more concerned about your success than you could ever be worried about it. He so wants you to depend on Him that He has designed you to need sleep while He has no ability or need for such a thing. This type of success is a reward for righteous living, He will help you. How will He help you? By manipulating the hearts of people to like and want what He has given you to produce.

Romans 9:17, 18 states, "[17] For the Scripture saith unto Pharaoh, Even for this same purpose have I raised thee up, that I might shew my power in thee, and that my name might be declared throughout all the earth. [18] Therefore hath he mercy on whom he will have mercy, and whom he will he hardeneth."

God is the original spell-caster! He easily causes people to do His bidding, follow His will regardless of their intent. We have all seen products that we ridiculed, and without us contributing to that business, they became overwhelmingly successful. What you hated, God caused others in the market to like, want, and purchase, even what we boycott. God allows us to continue in business and thrive. You should do your homework even when you have been given a prophetic word or dream. Learn all you can; do all you can. Do not allow yourself to become anxious because you do not know how to create a business plan, or you don't know how to forecast; know that God is part of your equation and will work with you, work through you, and work for you. I am not saying a business plan is terrible, just do not allow the nonexistence of the plan to keep you sidelined. When you need it, He will provide someone to help you with its development.

BUYING CAN BE MINISTRY TOO

I want to introduce a new concept to the Body of Christ to help us identify what we do when we buy from Christian businesses. The term is businistry. There are various spellings of it across the Internet but they have the same general meaning. It is the understanding that because our companies are birthed from the Spirit of God or because we use part of our revenue to support Christian endeavors, we see our businesses as a ministry, too. We are not speaking in reference to non-profit organizations, which are a ministry to themselves and recognized as charitable organizations under the IRS Code. I am talking about for-profit organizations that pay taxes on their revenue, but understand God has called them to this business to affect His Kingdom. These business owners also feel the call of God to create non-profits and give proceeds from the for-profit business to the non-profit for missions, or they use part of their proceeds to support other charitable endeavors focused on by existing non-profits. Either way, it goes, if you purchase something from a businistry, you too share in that heavenly reward.

Matthew 10:40-42 states, "⁴⁰He who receives and welcomes you receives Me, and he who receives Me receives Him who sent Me. ⁴¹He who receives and welcomes a prophet because he is a prophet will receive a prophet's reward; and he who receives a righteous (honorable) man because he is a righteous man will receive a righteous man's reward. ⁴² And whoever gives to one of these little ones [these who are humble in rank or influence] even a cup of cold water to drink because he is my disciple, truly I say to you, he will not lose his reward." (Amplified)

Christ creates the connectivity of the reward system. He has established it as one big machine. We are accustomed to this in a church setting, but we need to become just as comfortable with this concept in a business setting, even though the company is paying taxes to the government off of their profits. We should do all we can to support Christian businesses that provide jobs, education, and other charitable works in our own communities. *We will share in the reward.* When we purchase goods or services from secular companies, that is a worldly marketplace. But when we consume goods and services from Christian businesses, that is a Kingdom Marketplace. It is the place where God is welcome, and He has no restraints regarding blessings because the Kingdom Marketplace is comprised of His children. This is where the blessing of Deuteronomy

28 can rest upon us. Everything about the market is ministry because it is Kingdom Business. Whenever a transaction benefits the Kingdom, it is not only business, it is Kingdom Business. This means that transaction was recorded by the angels and has the ability to produce a Kingdom benefit in your life and an eternal reward in the world to come.

Acts 2:44, 45 states, "[44]And all that believed were together and had all things common; [45]And sold their possessions and goods, and parted them to all men, as every man had need."

This is not a system that men govern, but Holy Ghost. We must be cautious as we are campaigning and advertising that a certain percentage is going to a charitable endeavor, but we plan to do something else with the funds. Integrity is a must. According to Acts 5:

> "[1]But a certain man named Ananias, with Sapphira his wife, sold a possession, [2] And kept back part of the price, his wife also being privy to it, and brought a certain part, and laid it at the apostles' feet. [3] But Peter said, Ananias, why hath Satan filled thine heart to lie to the Holy Ghost, and to keep back part of the price of the land? [4] Whiles it remained, was it not thine own? and after it was sold, was it not in thine own power? why hast thou conceived this thing in thine heart? thou hast not lied unto men, but unto God. [5] And Ananias hearing these words fell down, and gave up the ghost: and great fear came on all them that heard

these things. ⁶ And the young men arose, wound him up, and carried him out, and buried him. ⁷ And it was about the space of three hours after, when his wife, not knowing what was done, came in. ⁸ And Peter answered unto her, Tell me whether ye sold the land for so much? And she said, Yea, for so much. ⁹ Then Peter said unto her, How is it that ye have agreed together to tempt the Spirit of the Lord? behold, the feet of them which have buried thy husband are at the door, and shall carry thee out. ¹⁰ Then fell she down straightway at his feet, and yielded up the ghost: and the young men came in, and found her dead, and, carrying her forth, buried her by her husband. ¹¹ And great fear came upon all the church, and upon as many as heard these things.

Anannias and Sapphira did not give a tithe to the Church; they elected to help some of their brothers and sisters who had a charitable need. You read the Apostle Peter exclaim that it was not a man who was lied to, but Holy Ghost. They executed a sale for not just philanthropic purposes, but Kingdom purposes, with the option of giving whatever amount of their choosing. Selfishness and dishonesty filled their hearts, and they lied about it being the total sum of the transaction. Character is vital as we are reflections of Him in the earth. He wants us to transact our giving and our business with integrity. May I remind you of Abraham as he sought to purchase a plot for Sarah, who died? It was important to Abraham to be fair with the owner and not use his grief or community status as a way to bless himself. I really believe there is some glory here for The Church as God uses us to minister to countries and Christian communities that feel as if God has forgotten them. This is a viable way to store up treasure in Heaven as you partner with businesses and churches that work to leave a fingerprint on the Kingdom and the world. We must never forget the admonishment of Paul in Galatians 6:10: "As we have therefore opportunity, let us do good unto all men, especially unto them who are of the household of faith."

For far too long the household of faith has taken a backseat to all men. We will no longer forget that Jerusalem has needs, too, and by consolidating our effort in both ministry and businistry, we can effect change. Let's help one another by campaigning for Christian businesses one person at a time and one church at a time.

CHAPTER 10

 Restoring Paths to Dwell In

The Spirit spoke to me about a concern The Father has regarding many of our children. He said this to me:

"The Father is concerned for the seed of the righteous because their parents have not sanctified Him in the eyes of their children. They have sanctified Him in their hearts, but there is a disconnect between what they have been told and what they see. Many of the righteous seed have turned back from following Him because they attribute the poverty or lack of success of their parents to Him. But I am the Spirit of Truth, and I tell you the truth: This fault does not lie with The Father. No. The parents who have believed lies told to them by so-called leaders who required them to yield in areas that The Father had not required. The Father requires a yes from more than the mouth of His children. He is looking for those that will stand in the gap for a people that have come through great humiliations and know that He is a rewarder of them that diligently seek Me. I desired to love you and shower you with blessings, but you refused and embraced generational struggle. Now your children think evil of Me and have turned to the world, thinking I would not bless their success. I will restore these broken places. I will get the glory in this matter, too. Your children will celebrate Me and declare this is the Lord's doing. I care, and I will restore!"

Isaiah 58 immediately came to my mind. Isaiah prophesied in that chapter that a time would come of emptiness and replenishing or restoration. We understand from that passage that things can go from barren to fruitful to scarcity to the restoration of the most profitable of those times. These seasons happen at God's discretion. Any thought that God is reactionary is from the pit of Hell. He declared of Himself to be the Almighty. He is not aspiring to anything. All He is, all He will forever be, is absolutely God. (I like to remind my church that God is not His name but job title!) Too many members of the Church believe God is soft, malleable, or indecisive. To the contrary. He is none of those things. If by chance you actually see those things in His Church or in the world and you think God is not powerful enough to bring order or clarity, know it is only a part of a master plan He is working in that area of your visual concentration. He still takes foolish things to confound those who think they are wise. If He allowed an area or system to fail or experience a reduction in capacity, it is for a reason. And contrary to many of those who think otherwise, He is not obligated to make you aware of any of His strategies; the just still live by faith (Hebrews 10:38).

It is more important for us to know what we should do when we see individuals, groups, communities, or even nations that experience emptiness or waste places after they have called on the name of the Lord. Our job and our responsibility, is to make those places livable and prosperous for the restoration of generations. How does that happen? Initially, we encourage them to seek God for businistry related ideas.

We help them initialize the process. We trade with them. And then, we watch God bring the increase. Pastors and other church leaders have gotten this wrong for years. We have even oversimplified giving. I believe in the giving principle found in Luke 6:38. "Give, and it shall be given unto you; good measure, pressed down, and shaken together, and running over, shall men give into your bosom. For with the same measure that ye mete withal it shall be measured to you again" (KJV) But that is not the only vehicle through which God will move. God gives us visions and ideas. We implement those visions and ideas, and He blesses them. How does God bless them? By causing people to want our goods and services.

Again, there are segments of the Body who think this truth is a deception because of their financial success or willingness to live without what they call the world's riches. If that is your belief, do not make that belief or opinion universal. God gives people the desires of their heart when they delight themselves in Him. Also your experience is not the only one made available to everyone. Jesus told the blind men He would do whatever their faith could believe (Matthew 9:29).

God makes promises, and God keeps His promises. The initial promise of prosperity came to Abraham, and he walked in its manifestation. Over time, the children of Israel were brought into captivity and made slaves against their wills. That poverty did not nullify the promise that God made their fathers (Abraham, Isaac, Jacob). Still, it did cause the promise to hover over them until God was ready to restore and rebuild the foundation of many generations. Some people struggle with disenfranchisement because it may not be universal or even pervasive, as they see it.

As I forestated, your experience may not be the experience of people who worship with you, work with you, or who may even be in your family. We have a tendency to tribal ourselves based on race and economics. How disconnected are some of us from the realities of others who we go to church with or simply live within twenty miles? How many people are we associated with regularly but have never asked them their story? We are notorious with the wave and go.

I think at times, we are all guilty of not wanting to breach someone else's space, but to be an effective worker in the Kingdom of God, we must be willing to know people on a personal level that affords them the liberty of sharing their hearts. That's how we know in what manner the Kingdom should serve them. There is a critical observation we miss continually when reading the Scripture as it speaks about the children of Israel in Egypt. They were in generational slavery. By the time Moses is sent to deliver them, they do not know God as Abraham, Isaac, and Jacob did. They did not have the Torah. There was nothing to reinforce faith in God other than the elders and their stories about God. The establishment of Israel as a nation was grueling. Yes, forty years is a long time to wonder, but think about all of the people who died because of rebellion and unbelief. Yet, it did not deter God because He made a promise.

The power of God will work both with you and on your behalf. Faith without works is still dead. Even though God will extend great mercy to many of us, He requires us to be actively involved in the work that we do, and He will bless it. Just as He did with the nation of Israel, He speaks to us:

Deuteronomy 28:12 states, "The Lord shall open unto thee his good treasure, the heaven to give the rain unto thy land in his season, and to bless all the work of thine hand: and thou shalt lend unto many nations, and thou shalt not borrow."

God promised the children of Israel He would bless everything their hands planted, harvested, manufactured, created, and produced. What a promise. It is clearly not an action that man can produce by the will of men because we are all subject to the laws that governs the earth set forth by the Almighty Himself. Only Jehovah can make such a guarantee.

If He spoke it, He will make it good. The only things He requires of us are to love Him, keep His commandments, and put in the work. He will take care of all of the rest. I need you to understand this well. Our Kingdom is not of this world. God is capable of blessing us, keeping us, and protecting us in the midst of challenging times.

God is strategic in His blessings that He can bless one and not the other. Two can be in bed; He can take one and leave the other (Matthew 24:40). What God does through you and to you is not the concern of anyone else, even though they may express opposition. But if God be for you, He is more than the world against you (Romans 8:31). You are not obligated to run the plans of the Lord concerning your life by anyone else, even though they may not like the plan God has for you to bring you to the hope and future He has thought of for you. Expect and live in the strategy of God, and allow Him to manifest His will concerning you.

Another point to make concerning restoration is the need for spiritual discernment to recognize the dogs and swine in our lives and those that are on the way. The demonic nature of Satan is first to steal.

Often, these beasts show up in people's lives for the sole purpose of separating them from their wealth and riches. Sadly, because of immature thinking, believers can give or sow into these people and organizations only to find out there is no appreciation for the seed planted or the gift given. Not only is there no appreciation, but there is also a reviling and spirit of destruction that comes upon them towards the person who gave it.

Matthew 7:6 tells us, "Give not that which is holy unto the dogs, neither cast ye your pearls before swine, lest they trample them under their feet, and turn again and rend you."

A fool and his money are, still today, soon separated (Proverbs 21:20). You must pray for wisdom and knowledge as you structure your business and in dealing with people. I believe in the principle of giving, but it is more important to be found doing so in the right places, being led by the Spirit of God and not the spirit of men.

The Church is in the midst of a season of restoration! Many of you have never experienced wealth and riches, but it does not preclude you from receiving from the Father. Your level of education will not be a factor either. The educated and the non-educated will need the power of God to work on their behalf. This too is not by power or by might, but by His Spirit (Zachariah 4:6).

Replace with: As we look at the world, we can see racial, social, and economic divisions–compounded by pride and arrogance–pulling cities, states, and nations a part. It matters not for us because our Kingdom is not of this world. The hardships of the world, from religion to politics to poverty, should be in place, as they prevent the world from experiencing bliss and coming into unity without the Creator. However, this should not be an issue for the Church because we are commanded by Apostle Paul to let brotherly love continue. We should all be preoccupied with the prosperity of our brothers and sisters in the Lord.

The last piece of restoration I want to share with you is the transference of wealth. It is a biblical concept with both spiritual and natural orientation. The transference of wealth is a reward to the righteous and a penalty for the unrighteous. It is a law set by God, enforced by God, and guarded by God.

We read in Ecclesiastes 2:26, "For God giveth to a man that is good in his sight wisdom, and knowledge, and joy:

but to the sinner he giveth travail, to gather and to heap up, that he may give to him that is good before God. This also is vanity and vexation of spirit."

Here is where we are. It is absolutely possible that God could cause unbelievers to give to you. The list is unlimited. It could be money, cars, houses, land, clothes, stocks, bonds, electronics, furniture, diamonds, and pearls, you name it. The Ecclesiastical writer says this is an action of God, all predicated upon the desire of God. There is absolutely nothing the sinner can do to resist it and absolutely nothing the jealous believer can do to stop it. If you can receive this, according to your faith, it can be done in your life. Your Christian education should include not only giving but also receiving. Too many believers are stressing financially because they only have a financial expectation that includes their work week, secular education level, and social security checks. You need to have an expectation of God rewarding you for serving Him. It is a reward that encompasses this life and eternal life in the world to come:

Luke 18:29-30 states, "[29]And he said unto them, Verily I say unto you, There is no man that hath left house, or parents, or brethren, or wife, or children, for the kingdom of God's sake, [30]Who shall not receive manifold more in this present time, and in the world to come life everlasting."

This passage does not speak to only extensions of family relationships or community living and community sharing, but the word "more" is the game-changer. It literally means much more. And the much more He is referencing is slated for this life and eternal life in the world to come. So too can a strong argument be made for Christ rewarding individuals as well for the sacrifices you have made for Him in this world that are tangible rewards. How? Because He said, you will receive manifold "more." The word "more" suggests an increase of ownership and not just community. The community can only experience increase through the efforts of the people and the blessing of God. Certainly, the young ruler does not expect reward because he was unwilling to part with his earthly possessions and would be the personification of the camel and the eye of the needle analogy. Remember Jesus said it is hard for the camel to make it through the gate, not that it is impossible. How long does it take to train a camel to change its natural state to perform this feat? Joseph of Arimathea could easily be the exception to the rule as Jesus articulates the possibility of a rich person making it into the Kingdom.

There are material rewards in the world to come for us, and there are material rewards in this world for us also. I cannot explicitly state the magnitude of them because they are based upon His assessment of us and our ability to manage the blessings of the Lord without them becoming an albatross to us.

Let me be clear on what is being restored; it is an economic engine fueled and managed by the children of God. The children of Israel were the original model of a community of believers with God as the nucleus (in worship, family, community, and business). What is being restored is more extensive and even better as it will consist of a Global Christian Commonwealth, made up of different blood, languages, and ethnicities – but one Faith (Ephesians 4:5-6).

Lastly, please do not allow your inexperience in the business world to limit or prevent your participation in the emergence of this new global Christian Commonwealth. The favor of God is your inheritance as becoming a son and daughter of His. His favor can get you started on the road of generational wealth for your family. I had a lunch with a cousin of mine one day, and she asked a question: How long would it take a person to fund their retirement if they started late in life? There was a consensus among the group it would never happen because they started too late. It is that type of thinking that can constrict the Body of Christ as we become more unified and self-sufficient. God is great, or God is not great. He can make all grace about toward you, or He cannot. We can do all things through Christ, or we can do some things through Christ. According to your faith, be it unto you. Be restored!

CHAPTER 11

Responsibility and Accountability

Now, the part that most people do not like: Along with wealth comes responsibility. The world has a saying that references the importance of drinking responsibly, not to the point of intoxication. This is for both the safety of the public and the individual who is drinking. Some media campaigns encourage the drinkers to appoint someone as the designated driver or even encourage the drinker to use a form of transportation that would take them home without cost. All of this because the combination of alcohol and a vehicle can result in deadly consequences. While I do not advocating drinking, this seems to be the perfect scenario to help us understand how being rich could result in fatal consequences for us if we are not purposeful, careful, and deliberate in our thinking.

By now, I am sure most of us have heard the saying, "Money does not change you. It exacerbates or magnifies who you really are as a person." Over the years, I have seen people who went from barely making it to instant wealth. Some of them because of sicknesses, accidents, or even a death of a loved one. Humbling events were the precipitating factors of this transfer of wealth, but humility was not a part of their true character. Once the dust settled and the check cleared, they became, or should I say, the real them showed up. I thought I knew them and would have lost the bet I made on them based upon what I perceived their heart's condition to be. They were not pleasant, sweet, kind, or easy-going people. The circumstances they lived, forced them to augment their behavior to survive their humbling situation. However, the moment their status changed, they had no need to regard anyone's feelings, did not need a ride, did not need to borrow money, the real them showed up. They were arrogant, belligerent, disobedient, disrespectful, obstinate, and then the money played out. What happened then? You can probably guess. They reverted to their former self. I didn't see this pattern one time. Not two times. Not even ten times. I have seen this pattern of behavior repeatedly from worldly people and those who confess the name of Jesus Christ.

Wealth is not something that is easily obtained. And generational wealth is a beast to tame. The discipline, consecration, and the fortitude it takes to generate long-lasting wealth are tremendous (if you want to do it the right way). The selfishness of such a heart coupled with such unethical behavior is unfathomable. The family history is such that wealth has alluded us and when the potential of generational life-changing wealth manifest's itself, all I can do is think about me?

That's terrible! Absolutely, terrible! Don't we owe it to our children and our children's children to help provide a better life for them or even an enterprise they can connect to in order to fill their personal coffers as they still work the family business? If you realize that you have not dealt wisely with your finances, that is a good thing. That is the best place for you to be as you seek to be a better provider for your family and the Kingdom. God is a forgiver of our mistakes and the best news of all: He has more than one blessing.

The story of the prodigal son is a comfort for us. Once we realize our pride and error, our Father, too, waits for our return so He can restore us. Learning the lessons of the Kingdom is essential for our continued growth and development as the Children of God. The Father is not in covenant with the world. He owes them nothing but a path to citizenship in the Kingdom through Jesus Christ. However, in order that we are safe, provided for, and recognized as a blessed people, God must always consider the source, power of the source, and His purposes.

Deuteronomy 8:18 states, "But thou shalt remember the Lord thy God: for it is he that giveth thee power to get wealth, that he may establish his covenant which he sware unto thy fathers, as it is this day."

The vision for the business, the strategies needed for implementing the plan (to bring the vision to pass), and the physical and mental strength required all comes from God. He gives us the power to get the wealth! Without God as a partner, all we would have is a vision. He knows, better than we do, the details that are needed to workout and manage the vision. We have no idea from day to day the challenges that we will face, and the endurance needed to continue in lieu of the adversity. God is the ideal partner as he can affect us spirit, soul, and body.

Why does God give us the power to get the wealth? God gives the power to obtain wealth as to establish His covenant with His people. God's desire is to be known and celebrated as the source of financial prosperity for His children, not their jobs. He wants it to be said that He gave us the power – *had it not been for the Lord on our side!*

We have heard it said, "Man makes plans, and God laughs at them." Well, you know whose plans are never laughed at? God! They may be scoffed at by wise people in their own conceit, but even that will turn into an egg on their faces because His plans will prevail. The most brilliant moves you will every make will be executing those directives given to you by God.

We must remember the faith requirement. Something that could be done in your sleep or without His assistance would not bring joy to Him and would not reap the kind of returns you are looking for. Many college graduates must often work in fields outside of their major. Not because they want to, but because they heard the voice of the Lord instructing them, and they obeyed. People in the world do this all the time when it is financially lucrative. But a believer will do it even when they don't see a need for such a decision and cannot figure out how this will be a blessing.

Do the right thing with your wealth. God is not blessing you to go on trips every month, waste money at a casino, or even give it to people who He has not ordained as recipients. The Body of Christ has real issues across the world, and your financial disposition will greatly help these areas. I am certainly not saying you cannot partake of your wealth, nor am I saying your family should not benefit. I am, however, stating emphatically that you must have the resources available as He demands. This is not your time to shine or prove anything to a detractor.

Your will, even in this area, should be lost in God. We often use the passage of Peter and the sheet in Acts 10 to justify eating whatever we want, when the real point to be considered is the Father had to talk to Peter before the knock on the door because of his personal prejudices. That still blows my mind. Peter literally walked with Jesus, studied under Jesus, even saw a resurrected Jesus, but that was not enough to affect his flesh.

My, God! Even after being filled with Holy Ghost, speaking in a language he'd not studied, preaching the first Gospel message of The Church Age, and 3,000 people giving their lives to the Lord, he still was not able to subdue his flesh. It took a one on one with the Master to preempt Peter's arrogance. Our old man, too, is semi-comatose, waiting on an opportunity to show up, make a mess, and embarrass you and the Church.

You should think responsibly regarding your wealth. It should not be the first thing you think of in the morning when you rise. Neither should it be the last thing you think about before you drift off to sleep. It does not define you as a person. Nor will it defend you if you get into trouble. It does not determine your value as a person or believer. Money is a tool. Money is powerful. But money should not be your reason for existing. Manage your wealth responsibly. On the other end of the spectrum, being careless and frivolous can cause you to experience what I call a hole in your pocket. When you show ambivalence for the things of God, you open yourself up to money coming in and going right out as it decreases in volume and consistency.

Or He will simply cut you off altogether. Either way, you can expect an unfavorable judgment from the Father when you disrespect wealth. Always remember that wealth is a blessing from the Lord. You did not luck upon it or stumble across it. God deliberately chose you to receive financial abundance. Show Him your gratitude by always being a good steward. God assesses us.

I do not know the reasoning behind not hearing more about the importance of doing well for the purpose of godly increase. God does not pull numbers out of a hat to see who is next. The process is not arbitrary in the least. God chooses people based upon what people have done. Not simply the potential, but actual fruit. And no matter how much we cry, beg, and yell, He will not move until He sees real work and consistent work from us.

Matthew 21:43 states, "Therefore say I unto you, The kingdom of God shall be taken from you, and given to a nation bringing forth the fruits thereof."

As He speaks these words to Israel, He has already judged and deemed them unworthy. He does not shut down His plan but rather has already pre-selected the next group that He will endeavor to receive fruit. This passage is extremely important for our information because it clearly conveys God's prerogative. We have forgotten that the earth is the Lord's and the fullness thereof, the world and they that dwell therein (Psalm 24:1). We have forgotten that He sets up kingdoms, and He tears kingdoms down (Daniel 2:21). All after the counsel of His Own Will (Ephesians 1:11). The Father assesses us to see how things are going and if there should be any substitutes.

We are here because there are rich families (righteous and unrighteous) that have not done as they should, and God takes the wealth from them and gives it to another. There are business owners who have been faithful for many years; there are also those who have not been faithful but oppress and rob the people. God has found them wanting! The consequences are sure. Non-negotiable. It happens in every industry you can think of; He takes from one and gives to another based upon His equitable discretions. All of the Lord's judgments are righteous and true (Psalm 19:9, Revelation 16:7). You should remember that because as He found them wanting and took from them and gave to you, the same thing can happen if you find yourself to be the obstinate, rebellious one. He will take you out of the game to warm the bench, and if need be, strip you of your uniform, and restrict you to the stands to be a spectator. God assesses us, and God replaces us.

ACCOUNTABILITY

It is not a strange thing that the One who is responsible for giving us the power to obtain wealth is also the same One who will review our accounts. For some insane reason, many believers find it troubling to read the book of Revelation. However, there is a verse that gives insight into one of the major operations of angels as they relate to both believers and unbelievers.

Revelation 20:12 tells us, "And I saw the dead, small and great, stand before God; and the books were opened: and another book was opened, which is the book of life: and the dead were judged out of those things which were written in the books, according to their works."

Contextually, this verse in Revelation speaks to the former inhabitants of Hell, the dead from the days of Adam through to the millennium reign of Christ. The saints that lived from the time of Adam through to the end of the Church Age works would have been judged, and they would have received their rewards and eternal appointments. The most interesting part about this verse is the revealed details of how God keeps records on everybody. Every word that is said, every deed that is done is documented. Everything we do is written. After all, did not Jesus say we would account for every idle word spoken? (Matthew 12:36) How could that happen if every word that was spoken were not being recorded? Someone from the angelic ranks is always present, always listening, and always recording what is said and done. You are being held accountable now. How do you think the law of reciprocity works? The accuracy of sowing and reaping is all predicated upon the measure of that which is sow coupled with the heart's intent. The angels see what we can't, know what we don't, and document it all to initialize the return process.

In Galatians 6:7 we read, "Be not deceived; God is not mocked: for whatsoever a man soweth, that shall he also reap."

Accountability in the Kingdom consists of a systemic approach by God to ensure that all His people get the returns He promised. Documentation of our actions, like His written word, makes us accountable. My wife is an educator and has worked in administration. She lives by an axiom, "If it is not documented, it did not happen!" I am reminded of the copious and detailed notes taken by people following meetings where they considered inappropriate communications to have taken place. And how off guard the individuals were when they had no documentation to support their recall of events, only their memories that proved fallible. The omnipotent, omniscient God documents everything. We would deceive ourselves to believe He does not have exact total recall, but yet He chooses to employ the angels to constantly follow us and chronicle our lives.

The question is, does He ever judge us during our lifetime on Earth? Yes. The previous verse we looked at in Revelation concerned events prior to the Eternal Reign of Christ. Let's look at a passage that will help us better understand the visitation of God during our lifetime.

Luke 13:6-9 states, "[6]He spake also this parable; A certain man had a fig tree planted in his vineyard; and he came and sought fruit thereon, and found none. [7] Then said he unto the dresser of his vineyard, Behold, these three years I come seeking fruit on this fig tree, and find none: cut it down; why cumbereth it the ground? [8] And he answering said unto him, Lord, let it alone this year also, till I shall dig about it, and dung it: ⁹ And if it bear fruit, well: and if not, then after that thou shalt cut it down."

Parables are essential to the life of a believer because they teach us how Heaven works. They give us a glimpse into God's character and give us a working knowledge of His great expectation of us. It is in this brief parable that we gain an understanding of godly assessments. While we work, He comes to check our output. It is within this short parable the psyche of God is revealed toward the Church. In days past, He was strict with Israel. He will be patient and caring with us. He could have instructed that fig tree to be removed the first year he came and noticed its barrenness. By the third year, He is appalled and wants it cut down. He is rich in mercy, and gives in to the gardener as he seeks permission to give that barren tree some one-on-one attention.

God will not endure with us perpetually regarding our mishandling of the wealth He is solely responsible for giving us the power to obtain. Accountability is not something that will start once the wealth comes. You are held accountable right now in every area of your life, e.g., church, marriage, family, health, job, and finances.

In many of our cases, the mercy of God qualifies us for this righteous and rich blessing. It is not our past stewardship, but Him choosing to bless, choosing to favor us. Don't get it twisted, though. He will still require of you what is required of everyone else who is righteous and rich.

He will have angels document your actions and report back to Him concerning how you are doing with this new and improved quality of life. His omnipotence affords Him the ability to create a set of circumstances or sequences of events that will bring wealth to you. If adverse reports are made about you because you mishandle the wealth, that same omnipotence will create a new set of circumstances or sequences of events that will lead to the degeneration of your wealth.

The conclusion of the chapter is obvious for all: Remember that your adversary, the devil, still goes to and fro seeking whom he may devour. If you can stay accountable to the Spirit of God and the Word of God, you should have no problems being found favorable in the area of your finances. You are not the king or queen of the block. He gives you the power to obtain wealth for the sole purpose of having streams through which you can serve others. Always keep in the forefront of your mind that Kingdom operations happen to us without our permission and without our ability to alter them. Many of you who read this book will have wealth and riches in your homes because other brothers and sisters in the Body failed their assignment relating to wealth and riches being in their homes. Where once God trusted them to give His servants meat in their season, they became harsh, brutish, and neglectful. Now the tables will turn in their lives. Where they once dealt the bread, they will need bread dealt to them. Warning: Don't become what God has now called you to replace.

CHAPTER 12

Why Rich Righteous Believers are Needed

Jesus did not preach the Church or Christianity. According to the Scripture, Jesus preached the Kingdom of God:

Luke 16:16 states, "The law and the prophets were until John: since that time the kingdom of God is preached, and every man presseth into it."

There is a sphere that includes both the visible and invisible, where God rules without opposition or hesitation. His Word and desires are carried out in this space, and He reigns as All In All. Indisputably, He is God. No one seeks His power. No one seeks His throne. And no one resents Him being God. He is loved and cherished.

The Kingdom of God is made up of all of His sons and daughters. Christ brought about this unity:

Ephesians 3:14 tells us, "[14] For this cause I bow my knees unto the Father of our Lord Jesus Christ, [15] Of whom the whole family in heaven and earth is named."

We are one with the Godhead, the four beasts before His throne, the elders, the angels, and every spirit that works on God's behalf. In Christ and through Christ, we are one. Though our destinies may differ, as our gifts and talents do, our purpose is the same: Jesus being the essence of every prophecy spoken (Revelation 19:10). If it will not benefit Him as He works through us in our generation to subdue all things (1 Corinthians 15:28), we don't do it! Our glory is not in ourselves but the Holy One of Israel (Isaiah 41:16).

The Kingdom of God rises in our generation as it has in no other, not even the early Church. We are a part of the crescendo that will climax with the Holy City's decent and eternal suspension between the new earth and the new Heaven for all inhabitants to see. Previous generations have all but lived dormant as they await the call that awakes the Church: The Bridegroom is coming, go out to meet Him (Matthew 25:1-13). According to this prophetic parable, half of the Church will awake as complete fools. I am careful to write these words. I need you to know that this season is meant to be a time of pre-separation and not inclusion. God calls the Church out of Her slumber that she may be seen making preparation to meet Her Christ. According to this prophetic parable spoken by Jesus, The Church awakens to a great time of synergy. All of the wise virgins do the same thing, all of them have the same answer for the foolish virgins, and none of them run after them; this is a different kind of Church. It is not emotional but strategically intelligent.

Much of our evangelism is oh, so wrong. We go out and share Christ with a nomadic attitude. The Early Church created systems, but they did not have all of their information. Remember, this is a critique. Israel forgot their roots, their past. Everything about the original Covenant was not wrong. He initially gave them an economic floorplan that would cause them to be a global financial powerhouse. They got this part right: be your brother's keeper. They sold land and possessions to share with those who stayed after Pentecost. But, they did not continue with the process of buying and selling among one another, much like they had a business meeting to replace Judas when Jesus instructed them to wait in the upper room until they had been endued with power from on high (Acts 1:23-26).

As the Kingdom of God rises, He must make a difference between clean and unclean, between holy and unholy, between the wise and the foolish. He must set us apart for His use and His glory. We continue to miss this fact of the Early Church, on the Day of Pentecost, the people did things they had no prior experience in doing. Yet, with all accuracy and zeal, they yielded themselves to the will of God and birthed the New Testament Church. Their number grew from an impressive 120 to a mind-blowing 3,120 within days (not including those who did not make it to the upper room). That is the type of success we can look for with the Spirit leading us and not us leading Him. Prepare yourself for the rise of the Kingdom of God as He moves throughout these individuals and leaves the others who refuse His will and way to their own fleeting devices.

Why do contemporary Christians try to live a Christian life before God without acknowledging our Faith's progenitor? Abraham was born out of season-long before the Church age. But, you can take his life, superimpose it upon a Christian, and it would virtually look the same. His faith justified him. It took Paul to help us understand the whole Abraham connection and the Abraham model. Even some pastors look like the Pharisees and Sadducees when they try to comprehend the importance of and relationship with Jesus and Abraham. Let me see if I can bottom line it for you: God sent Jesus to die for us in order for us to inherit the power of the Holy Ghost to continue the legacy of Abraham as the friend of God. When Jesus told the disciples that He no longer called them servants but friends, that is an acknowledgment of the original friend, Abraham. Jesus said servants don't know their lord's will, but the friend does. Did not God say to Abraham, "Shall I hide from Abraham..."(Genesis 18:17-18)? Jesus treats them like God treated Abraham.

You can take the faith of Abraham, and it will fit seamlessly in the Church Age. That brings us to this point: You shall be a blessing. That is what God told Abram before his name change. We often hear about God making him a great nation, making his name great, being a friend to Abraham's friends and an enemy to his enemies. Abraham has no control over God's response. This is where Abraham needs to focus his attention:

We read in Genesis 12:2, "And I will make of thee a great nation, and I will bless thee, and make thy name great; and thou shalt be a blessing."

God tells Abraham that he will be the source of good opportunities happening in the lives of other people. God tells Abraham that people will benefit more from his life than him receiving from them in his life. Abraham would be known for his generosity and not for being selfish. He would be known for blessing people and not for taking advantage of people. God set this man as a pattern for us to follow in faith. Before He set the pattern for us, it was tested, tried, and proven for our edification. It worked well. God used him and his natural son to show us types and shadows of things to come. If you need to know what to do in the Church Age, use the faith model of a man born outside the Church Age. He had perfect faith. This is faith that is capable of always trusting God, even in his giving. Let's remember one thing: God elected to have Moses spiritually see the days of Abraham, and selected what He wanted Moses to communicate to the people in the Book of Genesis. Had Abraham chronicled his life as some other biblical writers, we would have a greater base of information on the day-to-day life of father Abraham. We have what we have, and I believe it is enough for our journey into wealthy living. We must be a source of good opportunities for the lives of other people.

As we prepare to end this book, this chapter, "Why Rich Righteous Believers are Needed," does not include all things but it gives the proper perspective concerning why rich believers are needed. I do not hesitate to use the word needed. If this suggests there is an imperative, it is. I have often wondered what Bible white American supremacists read as they attended Sunday morning worship before a three o'clock lynching. I am sure they had selective passages to read and hirelings to preach what they were told to help the participants avoid conviction by the Spirit and their own self-condemnation. There are people who do the exact same thing today. They give to the projects they feel comfortable with while ignoring the sensitivity of Holy Spirit as He prompts them to support endeavors they detest without real cause. Salvation is not the only objective. After salvation, then what? There are people in need of a diversity of opportunities because the world has created a system that rebuffs them, oppresses them, or restricts their success. This is why righteous and rich believers are needed in the world.

God has always spoken to a people to inform them of pending judgment, doom, and blessings (Acts 11:28). We have no idea what group, what people, what nation He has told to prepare themselves for a better life.

In too many Pentecostal circles, Holy Ghost is only used for celebrating God and impressing one another with His gifts. The Book of Acts tells us one of the first movements of the people following Pentecost was making sure everyone had all things in common. It went a little farther with them selling land and placing the money at the apostle's feet for distribution among the Church. This is the work of Holy Ghost, too!

It is the epitome of arrogance to think we know the mind and the will of God. Creating nice comfortable boxes for Him to dwell in may be good for us, as we are not natural creatures of change, but it does not work well for Him. We must maintain a praying spirit as we walk with the Lord as He is known for doing things without our permission or a consensus of the Church. Some projects can be unusual or extreme and it may take a few years to normalize them within the minds of people. That's okay. God is faithful to His children. How He decides to meet their needs is at His discretion. There are always economies within economies. That is nothing new. The Church must prepare itself for restoring paths to dwell in that have been previously made null and void by God.

A project can be financially massive, but God may decide partnerships are not what He wants. He wants one person to meet the need. God does not have to explain to us why He is makes His decisions. Our job is to obey. Think of a water system in a region that is built to supply clean water to an area. Creating marketing materials to send out to prospective investors and waiting to hear their response on the prospectus is not always the most expedient way. What about a believer who is righteous and rich that can make it happen? Some will say it is not necessary, they can wait, or they should pray for rain. You may think those responses are silly, but they are also real and must be circumvented.

I was in Sierra Leone in April 2019. The president, Julius Maada Bio, is a born-again believer. There is a significant Christian population there, but the Chinese have their fingerprints all over the nation. I saw a communist country helping a country ravaged by war and disease with its infrastructure. The poverty I saw shifted my paradigm concerning how abject poverty really looks. It broke my heart to hear the people vocalize the grief of not having enough resources to register on the American radar, knowing this country of ours has the best engineers in the world and money to waste. They could help the people, by helping the nation of Sierra Leone recover from its devastating past. I know of another pastor in Uganda who also had to deal with adverse economic challenges but continued to preach Christ to the people. She would come to the states to preach, and the churches would sow into her ministry. She took the finances back to help her church. She continued to do this for many years.

She stayed in our home during her time in Houston and shared many stories of struggle and triumph. She told us of dump trucks that went throughout the community to pick up people to bring them to church because it was far for them to walk.

As I lamented over the transportation, she said, "You can hear them singing joyous praises to God as they come down the road."

She told us of how many people don't have beds, and during the rainy seasons, they sit in a church with no roof, sing praises, dance before the Lord, and listen to the preached word for hours. During her last trip to us, she asked if we would help build a church with a roof to keep the people from sitting in the elements. We were able to fund the church's construction, but we were not able to do anything about the living conditions of the people. I find no joy in this; I cannot be comforted,

I have no opinion about my country which refuses to find value in human beings unless they bring something to the table. It is not relative because my Kingdom is not of this world either. I do not take issue with people, even Christian people, who turn a blind eye. We will all have to stand before our Maker to give an account of the deeds done in our bodies. He is still the Righteous Judge. However, for those who would stand in the way of someone else as they work out their soul's salvation in developing the plan that will give them the best advantage to complete their earthly assignments, and for those who seek to hinder the work, I have zero tolerance. If you have a righteous unction that speaks riches to you for fulfilling your life's mandate, follow your heart and let the God of the universe pack you with blessings that will yield earthly riches in your life.

Use all of your power and strength to build a consortium that centers around you or the business that you are doing to net the profits you need to do the work of the ministry. Like me, you need to have millions and relationships with other millionaires, righteous and rich believers, to assist in developing the nations with Christian governments and others with pockets or regions of believing saints. Apostle Paul encouraged us to do good to everyone but always be on the lookout for the household of faith (Galatians 6:10). That's what time it is. Sowing into a Christian community in an ungodly nation at the behest of God can turn a government to Him, and cause a country to be reborn. Simultaneously, as you run your businistry, you get to employ those who don't only need a job, but those who also need Jesus. Corporate America has embraced the antichrist spirit. Many of our churches have also by getting in bed with political parties. God still has His own economy, His own Kingdom, and He does not need the world to support nor embrace it. He wants to show Himself strong and mighty (Psalm 24:8).

Many of you have absolutely no idea if you were one of those believers God destined to be righteous and rich because, like me, you were born in the belly of the beast. You are a part of a global system that works to suppress, dominate, and control its population. The idea is antichrist. Through its own demonic communications, hell is able to manage its kingdom and influence the Church. We must be spiritually discerning of our preachers, teachers, musicians, and christianpreneurs to live in the promised realm of Jesus where the gates of hell do not prevail against us.

I give you permission to pursue your destiny in God, free from the guilt and condemnation that comes from people who do not know the instructions God has given you to be a blessing. I give you permission to spiritually turn over the tables of the church's money changers through prayer and hinder racial supremacists and elites (who come in every color), who think they know best for everyone.

Prepare yourself for the great distinction. The king's heart is still in the hand of God, (Proverbs 21:1) whether the king believes it or not. God will change government, laws, and people in this hour to meet the needs of those who have been abandoned and oppressed by the unrighteous rich. And, the unrighteous rich will see it but not have the power to partake in it. New millionaires and billionaires are destined for this hour, and there is absolutely nothing you, I, nor them can do to stop it. Lastly, if that is you, do not be ashamed of your heritage. You come from a line of righteous and rich fathers and mothers. It is only befitting that you are a righteous and rich son and daughter.

CHAPTER 13

 ## Children of Covenant

A human covenant (paper contract or oath) requires two or more parties to bind themselves together, based upon pledges or promises that will benefit all parties involved. A God-Covenant, however, is different. Why? Because we as mere human beings in the presence of such Greatness have nothing to offer to God of any intrinsic value. All God can do is look across the table at such destitution and offer a way out. We have nothing to offer outside of loving Him, obeying Him, and remaining faithful to Him; we have no stock, bonds, wealth, gold, silver, enterprise, influence, or power, more incredible than He has, nor comparable to what He has. Nothing. All we can do is receive. What do we have to offer The God of The Universe? God has everything, and everything belongs to Him (Psalm 24:1). This is precisely what He did with Abraham. There was no bargaining with God on Abraham's part: God offered Abraham something that he did not have, and he seized upon it.

God promises Abraham, among other things, to make his name great and supply him with natural and spiritual Children. The book of Hebrews affirms God's pleasure with Abraham regarding him and the Covenant:

According to Hebrews 11:8-12:

> "⁸By faith Abraham, when he was called to go out into a place which he should after receive for an inheritance, obeyed; and he went out, not knowing whither he went. ⁹By faith he sojourned in the land of promise, as in a strange country, dwelling in tabernacles with Isaac and Jacob, the heirs with him of the same promise: ¹⁰For he looked for a city which hath foundations, whose builder and maker is God. ¹¹Through faith also Sara herself received strength to conceive seed, and was delivered of a child when she was past age, because she judged him faithful who had promised. ¹²Therefore sprang there even of one, and him as good as dead, so many as the stars of the sky in multitude, and as the sand which is by the sea shore innumerable.

You are those stars. You are that sand. You are the living proof of Abraham's faithfulness to God. You are what the Hebrew writer called Isaac and Jacob: heirs with him of the same promise. You must begin to see yourself as an extension of the branch of Abraham. If it were not essential to be connected to Abraham, the Scripture would have communicated that to us. Jesus is not working autonomously or randomly. He works on the Father's behalf (St. John 5:36). Where did the Father send Him to work? He sent Him to the lost sheep of the house Israel (Matthew 15:24). Here it is: Who are the lost sheep of the house of Israel? They are Children of Abraham;

the Children of Covenant. Here is the faithfulness of God manifested for all men to see. After all of these years of Israel's disobedience and Covenant breaking, God sends Jesus to save the world, but to the Children of Abraham, first. All people, after that, who receive Jesus also receive Abraham by default because the promise was originally given to him. A person's salvation is not predicated upon their knowledge of Abraham, only Jesus Christ. But it could be another story regarding the Covenant. You must know to what you are connected to. God's Covenant promises are not for the world. He only owes them a path to salvation, Jesus Christ. If you don't want Jesus, you don't get the promises.

Be not dismayed because your eyes are opening, and you may be looking at years of misteaching or Bible study neglect. There is a critical interaction between Jesus and a certain woman that can help us understand the power of the Kingdom and the mercies of God.

Luke 13:11-17 states:

> "^{11} And, behold, there was a woman which had a spirit of infirmity eighteen years, and was bowed together, and could in no wise lift up herself. ^{12} And when Jesus saw her, he called her to him, and said unto her, Woman, thou art loosed from thine infirmity. ^{13} And he laid his hands on her: and immediately she was made straight, and glorified God. ^{14} And the ruler of the synagogue answered with indignation, because that Jesus had healed on the sabbath day, and said unto the people, There

are six days in which men ought to work: in them therefore come and be healed, and not on the sabbath day. ¹⁵ The Lord then answered him, and said, Thou hypocrite, doth not each one of you on the sabbath loose his ox or his ass from the stall, and lead him away to watering? ¹⁶ And ought not this woman, being a daughter of Abraham, whom Satan hath bound, lo, these eighteen years, be loosed from this bond on the sabbath day? ¹⁷ And when he had said these things, all his adversaries were ashamed: and all the people rejoiced for all the glorious things that were done by him."

Jesus clearly responded to the woman, who asked nothing of Him, based upon her pedigree. He introduces a truth that we are far from because she is a daughter, not a son (get free sisters) of Abraham. She should not be experiencing the condition that had her bound for eighteen years. Jesus invokes Abraham. I need you to stop and ponder this: His reasoning had to do with her ancestor that she had never seen. Because she had the natural blood of Abraham, she deserved to be healed. Jesus knew this truth, and without waiting on the group to catch up or agree, He exercised His power over the demonic spirit that had her bound.

The Kingdom is about to happen for many believers in that manner. You, too, have dealt with areas of great difficulty in your life for years. You have even resigned yourself, with the knowledge of the Kingdom, not to receive it during your lifetime, thinking that maybe it is for your children. You remained faithful in the things of God, but you have suffered under the Covenant. Not, so. There are a new set of circumstances and events that God has planned for you that will change the trajectory of your life and your seed's seed.

I find the criticism of the ruler of the synagogue appalling. The nerve of the leaders to speak when they lacked the ability to do anything to help the woman, but still use her to serve, is unfathomable. But, it is the nature of the beast. People don't mind you not having options and fitting within their world as long as they have the power. They need you crippled. They need you weak. They need you insecure. They need you confused. They need you poor. They can deal with you in that condition. They can manipulate you in that condition. But Jesus came to set you free. You must remember: if any hates you, they are adversaries of Jesus. Let Him handle His enemies. Don't curse them; pray for them that their eyes would be open, and they find their usefulness in the Kingdom as Paul did after his Damascus road experience. You keep your focus on the works He has assigned to you. If they persist in challenging the manifestation of the Kingdom, they, too, will be publicly humiliated by the same One who set you free.

Our existence is predicated upon our history. Not knowing or understanding that history, can result in us living a life that God never intended. Don't be too narrow-minded or ignorant to obtain it. One of the things that have concerned me regarding some of the preaching giants I alluded to earlier is how they were able to preach the gospel to the approval of many people but never given leeway to the Church universally. This would have inevitably denounced racism and inequality. To preach a holistic gospel or inclusive gospel looks like this:

"For by one Spirit are we all baptized into one body, whether we be Jews or Gentiles, whether we be bond or free; and have been all made to drink into one Spirit" (1 Corinthians 12:13).

"There is neither Jew nor Greek, there is neither bond nor free, there is neither male nor female: for ye are all one in Christ Jesus" (Galatians 3:28).

As you can see, it is not left to the preacher to come to the truth of Kingdom inclusion, but instead documented by Apostle Paul to take away error and guesswork. Thereafter, it is encumbered upon preachers to modify their thinking, followed by corresponding actions. Thus, if you are a gospel preacher, your script is virtually laid out for you. You cannot go back and revise what has already been hashed out by God. He has already spoken on this matter whether you like it or not. Hatred is a work of the flesh (Galatians 5:19-21). Have we forgotten that it is possible to experience spiritual conversion, Holy Ghost baptism, Kingdom appointments to preach or teach the gospel, and still have hatred (enmity, hostility) in our heart for those who God has accepted into His Family?

Acts 11:4-12 states:

> "⁴But Peter rehearsed the matter from the beginning, and expounded it by order unto them, saying, ⁵I was in the city of Joppa praying: and in a trance I saw a vision, A certain vessel descend, as it had been a great sheet, let down from heaven by four corners; and it came even to me: ⁶Upon the which when I had fastened mine eyes, I considered, and saw fourfooted beasts of the earth, and wild beasts, and creeping things, and fowls of the air. ⁷And I heard a voice saying unto me, Arise, Peter; slay and eat. ⁸But I said, Not so, Lord: for nothing common or unclean hath at any time entered into my mouth. ⁹But the voice answered me again from heaven, What God hath cleansed, that call not thou common. ¹⁰And this was done three times: and all were drawn up again into heaven. ¹¹And, behold, immediately there were three men already come unto the house where I was, sent from Caesarea unto me. ¹²And the Spirit bade me go with them, nothing doubting. Moreover these six brethren accompanied me, and we entered into the man's house."

Question: Why did God have to repeat the same vision with Peter? Peter said this happened three times. Why wasn't the first time enough for him to get the concept? Better yet, why did it have to take a special encounter with God for Peter to get it? Peter walked with Jesus, and studied at His feet, but Paul, who didn't learn under

Jesus, didn't need this type of intervention. Can you now see how some Christian leaders miss God in the hour? It amazes me because they have degrees in theology, but they didn't get an understanding. They don't believe in the workings of Holy Ghost, so God's encounter to correct their heart and ministry is off the table. How sad. This should give us all pause. Why? If Peter could walk with Jesus, be filled with the Spirit, preached on Pentecost to the saving of 3,000 people, and still need help with His belief system, how easy is it for us to ignore the Spirit when He tries to correct us? We must be conscientious about our faith because rebellion breeds rebellion. Deluded people believe they don't hate anyone because they don't mistreat people of different races or genders. But what do you call neglect? Since when has ignorance or turning a blind eye become the Kingdom standard for clean hands. Jesus addressed it like this in Luke 10:29-37:

> "29 But he, willing to justify himself, said unto Jesus, And who is my neighbour? 30 And Jesus answering said, A certain man went down from Jerusalem to Jericho, and fell among thieves, which stripped him of his raiment, and wounded him, and departed, leaving him half dead. 31 And by chance there came down a certain priest that way: and when he saw him, he passed by on the other side. 32 And likewise a Levite, when he was at the place, came and looked on him, and passed by on the other side. 33 But a certain Samaritan, as he journeyed, came where he was: and when he saw

him, he had compassion on him, ³⁴ And went to him, and bound up his wounds, pouring in oil and wine, and set him on his own beast, and brought him to an inn, and took care of him. ³⁵ And on the morrow when he departed, he took out two pence, and gave them to the host, and said unto him, Take care of him; and whatsoever thou spendest more, when I come again, I will repay thee. ³⁶ Which now of these three, thinkest thou, was neighbour unto him that fell among the thieves? ³⁷ And he said, He that shewed mercy on him. Then said Jesus unto him, Go, and do thou likewise.

In the script provided to us by Luke that many have received as truth with its canonization, Jesus declares that we are to model the behavior of the Samaritan, "Go, and do likewise." The Covenant we have with the Father approves us seeing to the needs of people who have experienced life calamities.

One more thing about Peter's vision: He said the Spirit told him to go with the men, doubting nothing. Doubting nothing! What was there left to question? The Lord visited him through a vision to help with his incorrect perceptions, not days after his trance, but literally seconds after it. There was a knock at the door. Instead of beasts, there were human beings who God had sent of whom Peter would not have before entertained. What is there left to doubt? It's that flesh in which we live. It will show up and betray us at any given time. The Kingdom made demands of Peter, and his personal beliefs, comforts, and preferences did not matter. Despite Peter's stomach-turning, the Spirit said "get with the program."

It's a lot easier and acceptable to be the damsel in distress than it is to be the one stuck in your feelings or intellect, or to be the stumbling block to The Church. If you remember your Bible history, Peter failed at this again when he visited the Church at Galatia. He was dealt a devastating rebuke by Paul, and called out for it publicly. Therefore, we must pray earnestly for those struggling in the faith because of prejudice and bias. The good news is their power can't stop us anymore, but we don't want them to lose their soul.

Father, please help us modify all of the deeds of our bodies, by confronting and changing our thinking that cripple our lives and Your Church.

The Covenant we have with God is not a predication of our pre-salvation mindsets. To the contrary. We were given precepts and a cross for our flesh when it rises against the precepts. The Father has awaken us to a new life that we may produce good works and not dead works (Ephesian 2:10).

The Kingdom has a consciousness that includes us and depends on us but it is not us. The consciousness of the Kingdom is Jesus Himself. He declares that all power in both Heaven and Earth has been appointed to Him by the Father (Matthew 28:18)

By the time information gets to us, it has already been vetted, approved, and legislated by The King; He only awaits the obedience of His subjects. The Kingdom does not wait for the approval of men! We are fallible, inconsistent, and undependable.

We are incapable of creativity and production at such levels. We do have a treasure, but it is in an earthen vessel (2 Corinthians 4:7), and Paul said it is due to the excellency of the power of God – not us!

The Covenant happens to us, and for us. We are not the power or the glory behind the Covenant. Jesus is the brains of this operation. The world will know it. The world will see His Church, in our generation, as He has declared it.

The Father has permitted darkness to come upon the face of the earth in order for the saving knowledge of Jesus Christ can be seen in all of its preeminence before the Great Tribulation. As evil as things are now, they will be considered glorious days for men once the Great Tribulation begins. Jesus said of those days, "For then shall be great tribulation, such as was not since the beginning of the world to this time, no, nor ever shall be" (Matthew 24:21). The darkness is sin, but The Church's banner–which is Christ–provides the Light unto salvation.

God has promised to visit and care for the seed of one man: Abraham. And that promise is yours by way of default because Abraham is your spiritual Father. Therefore, your bond with God is no stronger or weaker than the bond of Abraham's natural children. You could only be made an heir by the works of Jesus Christ, who was sent by the Father to provide eternal life to all of Abraham's children (both natural and spiritual). You are a Child of Covenant.

CHAPTER 14

Kingdom Federations and Coalitions

There is one last thing I must relate to you regarding the structure and models the Kingdom will use. I certainly don't think they are revelatory, but we must discuss the intent of our hearts within this divine realm. We are the Body of Christ. There is connectivity among us, a thread that binds us together that we don't think about often enough and we don't function in as we should. We talk about the omnipotence of God but we lack the imagination to substantiate our belief.

Imagine this: God views the earth, but this time He removes any existence of unbelievers. He only sees the members of His Church as they continue their regular schedules. How connected would we be? Would our only interactions be on Bible study nights and Sunday morning worship? Would He see any functioning institutions? How dependent is the Church upon the world system? Is it all we have for our own family and generational survival?

We can work together because the Church has survived as an organism and as an institution. With all denominationalism, ignorance, and misinformation, the Church has survived. The Spirit makes a demand upon us to work together among ourselves in every possible area.

A man once said to me, "Bishop, we are losing the culture," as if we were ever winning the culture. According to the words of Jesus, I shared with him, that is an indication or sign of His soon return. We cannot lose what we never had. Satan is the prince of this world (John 12:31), and Jesus is the Head of The Church (Ephesians 5:23; Colossians 1:18). They are two distinct entities with two different missions, and two separate cultures. Our mandate given to us by Jesus is to be our light as opposed to their darkness.

Some astronomers consider The Bethlehem Star as a convergence or conjunction of planets, reflecting light from the planets giving the allusion of a single heavenly body. When we work together amongst ourselves with Christ as the center (obeying His teachings), our light shines in the world. We don't have to make it shine; it just shines.

This unity that God calls us to is new to us. While it is steeped in the Faith, it's not a Sunday worship that He requires of us now. Our worlds have never overlapped and intersected as much as they are about to connect. We will need the Spirit of God more than ever as we interact with one another in ways we are not accustomed to interaction. We will need to dispense more grace, forgiveness, compassion, and consideration than any other time. We are guilty of being impatient with the wait staff, the salespeople, and will tell off the manager because nothing was there to remind us of our Christian character. But when dealing with Church people, that will not be that easy.

True story: A pastor's wife acted unChristian-like in a public setting about a situation in which she was correct but disrespectful and she would not let it go. Another pastor's wife, who the first one did not know, acknowledged her concerns and told her that her suggestions would be taken under advisement. That was not good enough for that first pastor's wife, and she continued her tirade. With no results from deescalation, the woman's name and her church title was spoken out loud for all to hear along with her concerns, once again, being taken under advisement.

The lady immediately stopped. She was then apologetic. But that was after the fact. People talked badly about the lady's behavior, her being a Christian, and a pastor's wife. Behaving badly is never condoned, but sometimes it can be gotten away in the presence of the right people. But God sees all! Yes, God sees all but God is more forgiving than people. People will make you pay for misbehaving. While the Bible teaches us not to be a talebearer (gossip), that has never stopped some Christians from telling what they heard with their own ears and what they saw with their own eyes; nor others from repeating that information.

As we develop new coalitions and federations, you must be aware of your behavior in order that you do not limit your success. You will see these people multiple times. Our numbers are not as great as the world. You don't know who you will need as a customer, client, or business partner. Let's act like Christ (and when necessary), in the words of my wife, "forgive quickly and often." Wisdom is the key. You may have to get creative when you do business because the prince of the world does not want you rich. He may have resigned himself to the fact that you will be righteous, but he may fight tooth and nail against your wealth. Here is what I mean. There are numerous legal and legitimate reasons to use an offshore company. (Please note that I am not an attorney, tax or otherwise. If you should take advantage of loopholes etc., please consult with an attorney first, preferably one who practices in the area of offshore companies.) There are countries where many of our counterparts have already set up shop. The Internet is your friend. Now, let's remember that we are reflections of our King, and we render to Caesar the things that are Caesar's and to God the things that are God's. We pay our taxes using the tax laws in our favor. There is always a way. Talk with tax advisors, and attorneys who can help you legally structure your business; doing so where you are far within the possibilities of legal and nowhere close to jeopardy. Remember your name and ask God to help you keep it good.

I wrote earlier about the current phenomenon of merging. Large companies must consolidate to keep up with more successful companies. The amount of money being paid for some of these companies is in the billions. Some of the merges of divisions and subsidiaries only make sense if one company was already housed in a building. Having two companies under one roof make more sense because it increases the bottom line, and make shareholders happy. There was a time when we purchased burgers and fries across the street from the gas station. It is now normal to buy burgers and fries at the same place we buy gasoline. And the model works. While dad gasses up the car, the family is inside ordering the food; and both are ready about the same time. The model has been perfected. It did take some getting use to, but who thinks twice now? It is a home run for the corporation because they are not paying double for rent, insurance, utilities, etc., and even marketing expenses are decreased. These are mergers or corporations from within. The parent company makes the money, but two of their entities must remain solvent to make it work. On paper, the companies are different. Their inventory is different. Their workers are different. Their models are different. But their ultimate goal is the same – making money for the parent company, all while sharing the expense of a single building.

As believers, we must be strong enough to do the same. We must see the Kingdom as our parent company. To jump-start many of our businesses, we will need to help share the burden. We will need to merge our efforts!

I became familiar with Black Wall Street (Greenwood Zone of Tulsa, OK) in the late '80s or early '90s. My cousin, Pam, is responsible for getting me hooked on technology and graphic designs. She was the first person to tell me about the Internet. If I remember correctly, her first account was with a company called Prodigy. We ran into one another at an Office Depot close to her home and talked for quite a while. I was intrigued by what she said. The Internet seemed so futuristic. Eventually, I acquired an America Online account (AOL) (which I still have to this day) and could not wait to exchange emails with Pam. She always sent the most interesting articles. One day, I received an email from her about Black Wall Street. The subject line alone had me. In case you haven't heard of it, by way of introduction, a recent CNN article states, "At the turn of the 20th century, the Greenwood District of Tulsa, Oklahoma, became one of the first communities in the country thriving with Black entrepreneurial businesses. The prosperous town, founded by many descendants of slaves, earned a reputation as the Black Wall Street of America and became a harbor for African Americans in a highly segregated city under Jim Crow laws."

After reading the original article, I sat at my computer in total disbelief. The thoughts of it being fabricated reverberated in my head. I searched the Internet to find other articles about this obscure and tragic event. Mind you, this was long before YouTube. You had to read your way around the World Wide Web back then. I kept asking myself, *why have I never heard about this before?* I didn't know what to do with the information, but I knew instinctively it was imperative to my future.

Over time, the tragedy of Black Wall Street faded in my mind, and gave way to the hope of the memory of what was. What *was* Black Wall Street? Black Wall Street was a consortium of eclectic businesses, schools, and churches any community needs to support itself and thrive. The community found a way to reciprocate itself many times over while still allowing for competition and expansion. Nobody was the only one on the block. There was more than one bank, more than one church, more than one cleaners, more than one doctor...you get the point. Many products and services offered outside of this zone were also offered within the zone. The people chose to purchase from those businesses within this Greenwood Business Zone.

Just as with Israel, America herself, and Greenwood, we can see the business model works. For years, I have tried to bring the Body of Christ together, as the early Church did, for community and commerce purposes. Business is not new. But, the Church doing business in our generation is new. The airwaves and social media have been filled with people criticizing the "African-American" Church for not supporting the community. When in truth, Church education lagged behind. We knew the Scripture but didn't understand the Scripture. Now we must make haste to perform those things that are our inheritance as many communities are now rising up to try their hand at financial freedom.

We must hurry. Satan plans to make us the facsimile by going before us. We are the ensample! Economic empowerment movements are happening all over the United States and other nations throughout the world due to racial discrimination, gender bias, and economic oppression by political parties. Some of these movements have celebrity power, facial recognition, and money. I saw this coming with the breakdown of the music industry. It is not as powerful as it used to be because it is still trying to determine where the consumer is regarding purchasing power and ability. Many people don't want to buy music; they would rather listen. There is still a buyer's market out there, but it is dwindling. With fewer record companies and the invention of the Internet, artists have turned independent, and many have had remarkable success. Also, because there are no colossal signing bonuses and a powerhouse record label backing artists for concert tours, they must branch out into merchandising and create other income streams. Many people don't know it, but this is precisely how the wheel turns in Hollywood. You want the breakout role in order for you to create a production company to chart your own success. Much of this success has to do with promotion and marketing: that face generating income for them. Ignorant and unsuspecting people buy into that celebrity's world not knowing they are but a means to the artists' economic end, funding a lifestyle that benefits that celebrity's close circle of family, friends, and business associates.

I don't begrudge them their success in the least because, economically, that should be what we all want. I am, however, pointing out to you that every economic empowerment movement—no matter what the mission statement says—is not purely driven. It is a means to survive or be the shot-caller. The problem with both survival and shot-calling as the motive is it is not pure toward those who align themselves with the vision. Celebrities now unify to "help" struggling communities empower their dollars by purchasing from businesses that are part of their enclaves. To whom is the enclave praying? Who are these businesses? To whom do these businesses donate? Who do I make rich?

We must have economic empowerment that is in and of the Kingdom, where everybody's vision is respected, appreciated, and supported. The Kingdom is too big for one person to hold such power. The lesson God wants us to learn from Satan is clear: too much power is a breeding ground for temptation even in the presence of God Himself. Our engines must stay totally manageable, or we will face the same temptation and fall like Lucifer. Our engines must remain transparent, honorable, and Holy Ghost filled as He alone can help us identify Achan (Joshua 7), Korah (Numbers 16), Ananias and Sapphira (Acts 5), Simon (Acts 8), and the false prophetess of Thyatira (Revelation 2:18-29).This is not a game. We have scriptural references for God judging His people (Old and New Testament) for how they mishandled money and power. We can't keep the House of God clean without Holy Ghost.

When I say we must hurry, that is not to cause panic or feed into your insecurity, but to shake you from your fear and shift you in your faith. We have no reason to fear because God is for us (Romans 8:31). Satan did not lose his spiritual gifts upon his expulsion from Heaven. He still has all of the abilities afforded an archangel. His spiritual perception is not lost.

He is more perceptive of times and seasons than we are without Holy Ghost. At every strategic move of God, the destroyer was there endeavoring to stop the Hand of God, e.g., Adam and Eve (Genesis 3), Moses birth (Exodus 1), the birth of Jesus (Matthew 2), persecution of the early church (Acts 8, 9), and the woman giving birth of Revelation (verse 12). He can see the plan of God better than us. Therefore, you must muster the strength to step out of your box, get out of your comfort zone, and let God work His glory through you to the saving of souls even in business.

The world has come to a troubling revelation again that where there is unity, there is strength. God said of Nimrod and the people, "And the Lord said, Behold, the people is one, and they have all one language; and this they begin to do: and now nothing will be restrained from them, which they have imagined to do" (Genesis 11:6).

Secular corporations merge, collaborate, unify their purposes, and find success. Great success. Competitors find ways to work together on ventures and develop new systems, products, and services that impact their bottom lines. We must stop focusing on the rich getting richer and focus on *how* the rich get richer. Partnerships are the key in this hour. The market is no longer stateside. It is global and you will need partners all over the world to generate wealth the Kingdom is in need. Through these partnerships and collaborations, God will move. Satan is a strategist, but he is not the Master Strategist. God doesn't play chess, He created chess. Tell me who has the advantage? Unlike Satan, Jehovah is omnipresent. Satan and his caravan must go to and fro (Job 1:7, 1 Peter 5:8), their power is extremely limited in contrast to their Creator, God. God will use His power to exploit the weaknesses of Satan and his kingdom. By the time they get to the appointment to prevent you, the deal will have already been signed and the system generating and the process working in your favor. He set stumbling blocks for you locally, but not nationally and certainly not internationally. While he may know the plan of God, he does not see the strategy of God. And like he failed to kill Moses and Jesus, he will also fail when he tries to kill your vision.

One last thing about partnerships: Motown! It was arguably one of the greatest African American record labels of all times. Barry Gordy was not only the founder of Motown, he was a songwriter, composer, and producer; yet those abilities did not make Motown what it was in those days. Neither was it simply a magnificent roster of artists. The secret to Motown's immediate success was everyone's ability to check their egos at the door and do whatever it took to make the label successful, which included singing background on another artist's song. Do you think you would see that today? No! Not even in the gospel music industry. Everyone is self-absorbed.

But look what those Motown partnerships produced, a worldwide phenomenon; classics that are revered today. Partnership! Those artists did not continue singing background, they did what was needed for the recording, and they went back to their headlining acts. They did what was needed to jump-start the label and the careers of their label mates. Let's follow that model and use whatever Jesus gives us to jump-start this Christian economic empowerment movement. Let's bring our gifts and talents to the aid of our sisters and brothers to help them launch and then turn around to purchase their goods and services while encouraging others to do the same.

I tried to find an annual total on church giving, but I could only find an article that references an article no longer available on Christianity Today's website. It placed the number around $50,000,000,000.00 (that number would reflect giving not enterprising dollars). Fox Business had an article showing the annual reports of some megachurches, and their numbers were astronomical. I can't verify these numbers, but if the church give half of that number, that means people already understand the power of the Christian dollar. We only need to create Christian businesses that are equivalent, not inferior to secular businesses, and redirect the people's minds to supporting the Kingdom.

I have laid out a thorough argument defending our righteous and rich patriarch, Abraham, and many of his bloodline who walked in his righteous and rich shoes. I even reminded you of a Covenant God made with Israel to give them riches and prosperity upon the obedience to His Word. I took you over the New Testament and showed you how Jesus benefited from a righteous and rich believer. He never asked him to sell everything and give it to the poor. It is time for you to go forth in your business enterprises to help bring the Kingdom to a new plateau.

It is time to give the preachers the time and space they need to stay with the Word and stop trying to keep the lights on. God is calling us to undergird this next phase of Church ministry. Inexplicable things will happen to you that will hinder your ego, and force you to tell people when they ask how you became successful? It is the Lord's doing! Great likability will come upon you, not for your personal enterprise or consumption, that the Kingdom of God can eclipse the world system again. Great mercy will come upon you for the continuation of the Covenant with a benevolent God who keeps His promises.

CHAPTER 15

Prayers

Father God, I come to you in the precious and powerful name of Jesus Christ. I confess my sins to you and thank you for the blood of Jesus that affords me right standing with you as He is all of my righteousness. I also confess that I have walked according to the prince and wisdom of this world as it relates to my financial wellbeing. I have allowed myself to be unduly influenced by those who set themselves as experts, but they lead me to limits, restrictions, and frustration. I now desire the manifestation of the thoughts you have kept in reserve for me in my life. I want your plan, your will, and your way. I confess that I am the seed of Abraham and that I have been blessed with all spiritual blessings in heavenly places. I now open my heart, mind, and life to receive the abundance that your Son, Jesus Christ, came to give me. Father, I desire to have a better quality of life for my family and me and to be a blessing to others. I ask you to keep me in all of my ways, that I want not or waste not. In Jesus' name. Amen.

Prayer of Deliverance

As I come before your Holy and Righteous Throne, Father God, I do in the name of my Savior, Lord, and King, Jesus. He is my precious Redeemer, I seek Your help in relieving me from every Satanic oppression. I belong to you, but yet there are areas of bondage in my life. I ask you to do for me what Jesus did for the woman with a bent spirit: Have mercy on me because I am a child of Abraham. Deliver me from the powers of darkness in any and every form which weakens my witness, my life, or my service to you. I want to be made whole. I believe in your supernatural power. I believe that you are the same yesterday, today, and forevermore. I ask you to be to me what you have been to my other brothers and sisters. I ask you to do for you what you have done for my other brothers and sisters. Invade my being with the power of your Holy Spirit and free me from the clutches of Satan and his evil whelms. In Jesus' name, I pray. Amen.

Prayer of Salvation

God of Heaven and Earth, I come to you and confess that I am a sinner in need of rescue from the penalty of sin. I have broken your laws. I have come short of your eternal glory. I ask you to save me and to write my name in the Lamb's Book of Life. I receive the eternal gift of your Son, Jesus Christ. I believe in your impossible and glorious work as He was born of a virgin, lived a sinless life, worked miracles, died on the cross in my stead, was resurrected, is seated at your right hand, and will soon return to set up an eternal Kingdom. I believe He is the only way to you. I am not ashamed to confess the name of Jesus Christ before human beings. I ask that You make me an effective worker in your Kingdom by clearly showing me what You want me to do and where you want me to go. Please help me to work alongside my spiritual family on the earth without causing controversy or divisions. Thank You for saving me and welcoming me into Your family. Lastly, Father God, please lead me to a Spirit-filled Church where Your Word is taught, and I have the opportunity to work out my soul salvation. In Jesus' name, I pray. Amen.

Prayer for The Church

I come to You, Father praying for the success of The Church. Our enemies are many, from without and within. I ask You to endue us with Holy Ghost power that we may both serve You and take up spiritual arms against Satan and his army. We cannot contend for the faith without the indwelling of the Spirit, His leading, and His communication. I pray that The Church will coalesce around Him and come under His Divine influence even as the early church did in the book of Acts. I ask you from this day forward that you would disallow any Satanic success against The Church as Christ stated concerning the gates of hell. I pray that all false workers, deceitful workers, and hypocrites be exposed, removed, and their influence in both The Church and the world be destroyed. I pray that your ministers would take up arms in lifting The Christ that He may draw souls to Himself once more. Lastly, I pray against all forms of denominationalism intended to separate and castigate us. We are still of one Lord, one faith, one baptism; with You above all, through all, and in all. Manifest Your power in our generation. What You do in one, I ask that You do in all. In the mighty name of Jesus, I pray. Amen.

Prayer for The Kingdom

Oh Lord, our Lord, how great is Your Name. You Father, are the Master Creator of all things, above the earth, in the earth, and below the earth. All things must bow to your Holy Name. I pray for the expansion of your Kingdom. Your Kingdom come, and Your will be done, Oh Great God, on Earth as it is done in Heaven. I pray that your majesty, power, and knowledge fill every space throughout the entire universe. I pray for the unification of all your sons, daughters, angels, and heavenly creatures as your Son prepares for war against Your enemies. I pray that you once again manifest your power among mankind that they may know that you alone are God. Grant us your might as we fight the good fight of faith. Help us stand with, and for The Messiah, You have sent to save those who will receive Him and to crush Your enemies. Your Kingdom come! In Jesus' name, I pray. Amen.

Prayer for Wisdom

Father, Jesus said the Kingdom is not of this world. I pray today that you would endow me with wisdom from on high. I pray that You would give me a natural intellect to understand and process information. I do not seek this gift for my glory but that You may be glorified in my life. As you still work Your divine plan of redemption, I pray that You will breathe on my understanding that I would have eyes to see, ears to hear, and a heart to believe. Your ways are not my ways, and your thoughts are not my thoughts. Please give me wisdom that I may serve You, well; that I may have a heart to ascertain the things Your Spirit would reveal to me from Your mind. I no longer wish to walk after the wisdom or prince of this world. Please hear my prayer and grant my request. In the name of Jesus, I pray. Amen.

Prayer for Witty Inventions

Father, I pray that You activate the creative spirit You have placed within all of your children. I pray that You inspire and stimulate the minds of Your children to create. Visit them with dreams and visions of things long conceptualize in Your mind that catapulted them into successes they could have never dream. Father, cause the minds of my brothers and sisters to be envied by the world, that they have an opportunity to sit on secular platforms and give You glory. I also pray that You will provide the funding they need to take the vision from idea to market. I ask You to be gracious unto them. I ask You to give them the mind to take existing ideas and improve upon them above measure. I ask You to provide them with eyes to see niches and inventions of necessity. I ask You to give them a calm and quiet place to perceive Your will for their business life. Lastly, I ask You to keep them from the spoiler, the fowler. Please make these days great for them and their families. In the mighty name of Jesus, I pray. Amen.

Prayer of Favor

Father God of all grace, I come to You in the name of your Son, Jesus. I pray now for the work of the ministry that must be done in His name. I ask You to do what is forbidden to us, change and manipulate the hearts of the people on our behalf. I ask you to cause them to favor us. The early church had favor with You and the people. I ask for the same in our generation. You said if our ways please You, You will make our enemies be at peace with us. Father, I pray for the surrendering of the hearts and minds of Your people to You wholly that we would have favor with people. I pray that You cause them to like us and speak well of us, even if they hate You. Cause them, Father, to not be hindrances in our great work for the Kingdom. Cause them to help, even if they don't want to help. The heart of the king is still in Your hands. Turn the king's heart in our favor that we may rebuild the walls of The Church, evangelize our neighborhoods, teach transgressors Your way, and build a global Christian commonwealth for the prosperity of Your people. As long as I believe, nothing is impossible with You. I ask this petition in the name of my great King, Jesus the Christ. Amen.

Prayer of Satanic Failures

All-Powerful God, I come to You in the name of my eternal King, Jesus. As He has left The Church in our care, I acknowledge the attacks of the enemy of our souls. I pray to You, Holy Father, All-Wise and All-Knowing, that You would cause the plans of Satan and his kingdom to fail and fail miserably. I acknowledge his time and space given by You to make war against the saints, murder, and of global deception, but it is not now. I pray, Father, that You will give us, Your Holy Church, power once again to tread on serpents, scorpions, and over all of the power of the enemy. I pray that You will equip us to win. Please give us the advantage over him and his kingdom, both naturally and spiritually. I know Your gifts and callings are without repentance, but I ask You to give us, Your Church, more power, more strength, and more of your Spirit; that we may help Christ subdue all things so You may once again be all in all. Jesus told us we would do greater works because He returned to You. Grant us the victory over all of Satan's devices. Bless every Christian agenda that is submitted to You, and curse every Satanic plan. In the potent name of Jesus, I pray. Amen.

About The Author

Born Edward Lee Johnson Jr., Bishop Ed is a native Houstonian. He is the son of Deacon Edward L. and Erma Johnson Sr. He attended M. B. Smiley High School, and Texas Southern University. He is the husband of Pastor Marilyn Johnson and the proud father of Chas Braxton, Christal Joi, Edward III (Tre'), and Kyle Maxwell. Bishop Ed is the founder and president of Ed Johnson International Ministries, which includes several ministries and conferences: Woman You Have Dominion Too Conference, Next Life Seminar, Church Music Symposium, Church Ministry Leaders Workshop, and more. He is also a certified Christian Counselor.

Bishop Ed is the founding and senior pastor of Christ Worship Center (Houston, Texas), serving with Pastor Marilyn for over 20 years. The ministry has seen its ups and downs, but the preaching and teaching of Bishop Ed have never wavered from the holy and sanctified living required of all believers.

Bishop is an accomplished singer, songwriter, musician, and choir director, appearing on stage with many renowned gospel artists throughout the years. In the early '90s, he formed a group called "Ed Johnson & Praise," which attained prominence with the original recording of "Where Are The Christians?" That year at the Texas Gospel Music Awards, they were nominated in three categories and won two; Group of the Year and Song of the Year.

Walking with God since the age of 9, Bishop Ed's fervor for God and the things of God has only grown through the years. He has spent hours in the presence of God, praying in the Word of God, and fellowshipping with the Spirit to prove the anointing on his life; it is evident once you hear him literally break the bread of life. He has also experienced great trials and spiritual attacks by the powers of darkness (spiritually and naturally) but has weathered every storm by the Grace of God.

He is known for his wise counsel: Frequently, he is found in private consultations with members of the five-fold, instructing them on church protocol, vision development, and spiritually discerning their house and ministries. He loves spending quality time with young pastors – preparing them for and encouraging them in this good fight of faith.

The love that Bishop Ed has for God is evident in the manner he handles God's people. He is constantly seeking ways to establish the people of God in the service of God. He is an ordained apostle, bishop, and pastor. He is an entrepreneur, published author, husband, father, friend, musician, visionary, and a man who loves and fears God. His life's mission is to prepare the Saints for the world to come.

www.ingramcontent.com/pod-product-compliance
Lightning Source LLC
Chambersburg PA
CBHW071426160426
43195CB00013B/1830